The Acquisition of the Holy Spirit in Ancient Russia Series
No. 2

SALT OF THE EARTH

Elder Isidore

SALT OF THE EARTH

or

*A Narrative on the Life of the Elder of Gethsemane Skete
Hieromonk Abba Isidore*

Compiled and arranged by his unworthy spiritual son
Paul Florensky

*Translated from the Russian by Richard Betts
Edited and annotated, with poetry versification
by the St. Herman Brotherhood*

ST. HERMAN OF ALASKA BROTHERHOOD
PLATINA, CALIFORNIA
1987

Originally published at
Sergiev Posad
Holy Trinity-St. Sergius Lavra
1908

Address all correspondence to:
St. Herman of Alaska Brotherhood
P. O. Box 70
Platina, California 96076

FIRST EDITION

Cover: *Elder Isidore in a moment of "prophetic seriousness" (see p. 80).*
Oil painting by Fr. Damascene.

Library of Congress Cataloging in Publication Data

Florensky, Saint Paul, 1882-1943.
   Salt of the earth.
   Translated from the Russian.
   1. Christianity—Orthodox Saints. 2. Russian Orthodox Church—
Saints. 3. Biography.
   I. Title.

Library of Congress Catalogue Card Number 88-060563
ISBN 0-938635-25-5

CONTENTS

CHAPTER 16

CHAPTER 17

CHAPTER 18

CHAPTER 20

CHAPTER 21

LIST OF ILLUSTRATIONS

INTRODUCTION:

St. Paul Florensky and *Salt of the Earth*

by Abbot Herman and Fr. Damascene

The only biography of the great Elder of Gethsemane Hermitage, Hieromonk Isidore, is presented here for the first time in English. It was written in 1908 by the Elder's spiritual son, the philosopher and theologian P. A. Florensky (1882-1943). While Elder Isidore belonged to the thousand year-old tradition of Holy Russia and could be called typical of the monk-saints of his time, Florensky was a very unique phenomenon. The latter was at once a mathematical genius who became famous in the fields of astronomy, physics and electrical engineering; a gifted poet, musician and art historian; a linguist and etymologist who mastered Greek, Latin, most of the modern European languages and those of the Caucacus, Iran and India; as well as an original theological thinker and metaphysician. He was a personality of such rarity that up to today he has not been fully understood.

1. FLORENSKY'S EARLY YEARS

Fr. Paul Florensky was born into an aristocratic family in Transcaucasia on January 9th, 1882. His father was an engineer of Russian descent, and his mother was Armenian. Although some of his father's ancestors had been priests, the young Paul was not raised in a religious atmosphere and was never taken to church. His first spiritual yearnings, therefore, were not the result of outside influences, but of an internal awakening to a higher reality. Through an experience of nature Paul began to feel awe before the unfathomable wisdom of God, the intrinsic goodness of creation, and the vastness of eternity.

Paul completed his secondary education in Georgia, where his remarkable abilities in mathematics became apparent. Upon graduating, he underwent a spiritual crisis that gave direction to his early yearnings. It was at this time, he wrote later, that "the limitations of physical knowledge were revealed to me." While before he had regarded science as the key to all the secrets of existence, he now realized that there was a level of existence it could not begin to reach. Interestingly enough, it was only after he had come to this conclusion that he felt free to use science in a practical way, within the lower—or material—order of being. "My striving toward the technical applications of physics," he wrote, "was instilled by my father, but was formed only when science ceased to be [for me] an object of faith. And later on, from that very crisis, came my interest in religion."[1]

Florensky enrolled in the Physics and Mathematics Department of Moscow University, graduating in 1904. By this time his conversion to the Faith of his fathers—Orthodox Christianity—had become complete, and constituted the most important element of his life.

As one of his contemporaries put it, Florensky's whole character became marked by "an inward revolt against the world." He could not help but detest prescribed norms which were determined according to the way the world thinks. He saw this as merely wearing a mask that makes one accepted by

1. Autobiographical notes of January 1, 1921.

everyone, dragging out a comfortable existence at the expense of selling out one's highest aspirations toward Truth. His rebellion against "standardization" and prescribed behavior came not so much from his will as it did from his very nature, which had been marked since childhood with a stamp of uniqueness.

2. ELDER ISIDORE

In 1904 Florensky enrolled in the Moscow Theological Academy, which was then under the direction of a great hierarch who was later to share Florensky's fate of martyrdom: Archbishop Theodore Pozdeyev.

While studying at the Academy, Florensky came into contact with a man who was to deeply influence his whole approach to Christianity and the spiritual life. This was Elder Isidore, then living in a little cabin on the outskirts of Gethsemane Skete, which was near the Academy. Many of the monks at the *skete* regarded Isidore as something of an eccentric. The educated class paid no attention to people like him, whom they looked down upon as mere unlearned *muzhiks* (peasants). It was largely Isidore's own fellow *muzhiks* who appreciated the simplicity of his wisdom and the abundant love—that highest of Christian virtues—which was at all times to be seen on his radiant face. Florensky, who most of all loved what was genuine and unaffected, saw Isidore in the same way as did the simplest villagers; but as a philosopher and metaphysician he was also able to articulate his impressions and find their source. "Asceticism," he wrote, "produces not a *good* but a *beautiful* personality; the characteristic peculiarity of great Saints is not the goodness of heart which is common among carnal and even very sinful men, but spiritual beauty, the dazzling beauty of radiant, light-giving personality, unattainable by carnal men weighed down by the flesh."[2] This can be seen

2. N. O. Lossky, *History of Russian Philosophy* (London: George Allen and Unwin, Ltd., 1952), p. 182.

as a direct expression of how Florensky regarded the ascetic Fr. Isidore.

In Fr. Isidore, Florensky also found an embodiment of his ideal of monasticism, an ideal characterized by *freedom of spirit,* freedom to live according to the laws of spiritual life, so vastly different from the ways of the world. Florensky, whom as we have seen hated all forms of role-playing, well knew that church figures were often much more artificial than laymen. Fr. Isidore, on the other hand, was at all times himself, in keeping with the ancient words of Socrates: "It is better to be than to seem." He refused to be governed by worldly codes of behavior, and broke them with charming ingenuousness. Absolutely fearless, he was at the same time possessed of profound humility. He was soft, warm, pliant and innocent—like a child, yet he could stand up to anything. For Florensky, Fr. Isidore— a lowly, forgotten old monk—was a giant who dwelt on another plane, a truly spiritual man who viewed things from a spiritual perspective and bore witness to the reality of the other world.

Fr. Isidore reposed in 1908; and, to pass on to others what he had gained from him, Florensky wrote the present book, *Salt of the Earth.*

3. MONASTIC YEARNINGS

The natural disposition of Florensky's character was strongly drawn to monasticism, but his spiritual father, the retired Bishop Anthony, advised against his taking this path. Bishop Anthony, a practical man and a shrewd observer of human psychology, spotted genius in Florensky—genius that might be subjugated and reduced to a common denominator under the rigorism of common monastic life. Florensky's inquisitive, analytical nature and limitless creativity were what moved him most of all, and were even more compelling than his monastic inclinations. Confining these impulses in a monastery, Bishop Anthony felt, would someday cause problems for Florensky's

personality, and thus he consciously diverted Florensky's energies into theological and scientific studies.

People speak of natural genius as a gift. As with natural beauty, our salvation does not depend on it, but rather on what we do with it. Florensky used his "gift" for his salvation by bearing it as a cross, since it was his very genius that prevented him from fulfilling his cherished desire of becoming a monk. It made it impossible for him to become "like everybody else," embracing the personal obscurity which monks should be seeking. But what a torture this was for him! The fact was, he *wanted* with all his heart to be like those simple, humble monks who go unnoticed by the world, never achieving outward greatness in anything, and yet pleasing God by the beauty of their quiet lives and so inheriting the Kingdom. But he could not change himself; he was different from the common lot. The words which he once wrote in reference to Pushkin could also have been applied very well to himself: "The fate of greatness is suffering from the external world, and inward suffering that comes from oneself. So it was, so it is, and so it shall be."[3]

As he bore the cross of rare genius, Florensky's suffering and tension only fed and strengthened his creative powers. He was compelled to find his longed-for monastic freedom outside the enclosure of a monastery, without the benefit of external monastic trappings, following an arduous path that eventually led to the freedom of dying for Christ.

4. SUFFERING

Florensky was elected to the Moscow Theological Academy's Faculty of the History of Philosophy in 1908. During his first few years of teaching at the Academy, he fell into severe depression. Many factors contributed to this: the death of his

3. Letter of Florensky to his mother from the Solovki concentration camp, 1937.

Elder Isidore, his not having entered a monastery, and his boredom with being trapped in a "standard" academic role, grouped together with scholars who had lost touch with the mystical Truth of church life. The cause of his problems, he said, "is a desire for something real, some kind of total contact, a guarantee of church life. I don't find this contact anywhere, only papers, never gold. I'm not saying that there's nothing gold in church, but I never find it. If I would not have believed, it would have been easier. But that is precisely the hard part: I believe there is contact, and if there is no contact, that means there is no Church and there is no Christianity. They order me to believe—and I believe. But that is not life."[4]

Thus, for Florensky, it was not enough to just go through the motions of church life, considering oneself and being considered by others to be a good, "churchly" person, experiencing the grace of the Church only vicariously, knowing that *others* have experienced it in truth and that it *objectively* exists. Florensky needed to know and feel it himself. As a teacher and writer, he wanted everything that came from him to be derived from the reality of his own experience. The most lofty philosophy had to be human, personal and living, not merely abstract and theoretical. It was his perseverance in achieving this, even more than his natural genius, that made him stand out among the thinkers of his age.

Valuable insights into Florensky's character at the time of his crisis have been provided by Fr. Alexander Elchaninov, who recorded the contents of their conversations. At the height of his inward suffering, Florensky told Elchaninov: "It is not difficult to kill much in myself, but what will be the result? I could have killed in myself everything connected with sex, but then my scientific creativity would have died within me first of all. You tell me that this is what should be done—that through such a death all the ascetics had to go. I know

---

4. "Iz Vstrech s P. A. Florenskim" ("From Meetings with P. A. Florensky"), *Vestnik* no. 142 (1984), p. 76.

that, but I'm not allowed to go to a monastery—they order me
to give lectures. Why is it that from many writings—textbooks
and so on, especially the seminary texts—there is a smell of
death? It seems that everything is there—there is great knowledge and decent language, even thoughts; but why is it impossible to read them? It is because they were written by 'eu-
nuchs.' And I could have written like that, but who needs such
writings?"[5]

In his misery, Florensky felt closer to God. "I am noticing
lately," he told Elchaninov, "that now some strange things oc-
cur to me. Formerly my prayer was never so strong as it is
now, when it seems I am least of all worthy. I get the impression that God deliberately goes out to meet me in order to see
what end I will come to. I sometimes have a strange feeling,
absurd from a theological point of view, perhaps because I cannot properly express it. —I even feel at times sorry for God,
that I was born such an evil one. . . . Yes, I can express it that
way. If someone gets very angry, then people begin to agree
with him and do what he wants. This is how God treats me
now. Of course, it is mostly in trifles. Yesterday, for example,
V. B. [who later became Florensky's brother-in-law] did not
come home even when it got late. I was very upset. The expected time passed—he usually comes in around 11 p.m. I was
terribly alarmed and began to pray, and hardly had I finished
praying, when he stood at the door."[6]

At one point, Elchaninov and Florensky spoke about a certain Bishop Gabriel. "Yesterday at our place," Elchaninov re-
cords, "[the Bishop] served, and I was amazed at the solemni-
ty and uniqueness with which he served. I asked Paul about
this. 'You know my opinion of him,' he began with irritation.
'All this sounds false and theatrical. He pronounces the words,
and one feels that the tone and diction are pre-planned, and
that he looks around at what kind of impression they create

5. *Ibid.*, p. 72.
6. *Ibid.*, p. 74.

on others. It is quite possible that objectively all this is accepted differently. But I know him, and cannot free myself from this feeling. He knows well the church service, he loves it; but this precision and this effectiveness—is not the Orthodox way of doing things. In you there is obviously a Westerner; and to us, just the contrary, the church service is dear when it's conducted as it is everywhere in Russia: they stumble, it is ugly, and so on. —We like the look of the slaves,[7] while you want even the *rags* to be unreal and have a silk lining. What I'm saying is evangelical, not just Orthodox. Why did Christ love so much the society of harlots and publicans? Just imagine—these were *real* harlots who would fight, conduct indecent talks, swear . . . and Christ preferred their company to that of the Pharisees. Just think, why is it said, 'The power of God is performed in poverty'? Poverty is not only weakness, not some poetic sickness like tuberculosis, but sinfulness, defilement. Christ was with sinners not only because they needed Him more, but because, for Him, it was more pleasant to be with them; he loved them for their simplicity and humbleness."[8]

Florensky's words strike a familiar chord for those of us in the West who would try to be Orthodox. Lacking the proper "feel" for the whole world of piety that has grown out of centuries of down-to-earth human experience in the Orthodox Church, we are all too prone to want our Orthodoxy looking "slick," to be attracted by outward glitter, correctness, precision. A kind of vain artifice attempts to cover up our emptiness. But our love of glitter may also result from the erroneous, deep-seated belief in progress—that, "after all, we mod-

7. This is a reference to a famous Russian poem (untitled) by Fedor Ivanovich Tutchev (1803-1864), which ends thus:

> Dear native land! While carrying
> The Cross and struggling to pass through,
> In slavish image Heaven's King
> Has walked across you, blessing you.

8. "Iz Vstrech s P. A. Florenskim," p. 74.

Top: New Martyr Priest
Paul Florensky (†1943).

Bottom: New Martyr Archbishop Theodore Pozdeyev
(†1935), who ordained
Fr. Paul.

Florensky in 1906, at the time he knew Elder Isidore.

Elder Isidore in 1906, two years before his repose.

Three spiritual preceptors of Fr. Paul Florensky.

Top left: Elder Anatole the Younger of Optina (†1922).

Top right: Archpriest Aleksei Mechiev (†1923).

Bottom: Elder Nektary of Optina (†1928).

erns are more sophisticated than those before us." To us Westerners, the "look of the slaves," the ugly, the poor, the insignificant—is often repulsive, or at least beneath our dignity. To the Orthodox mentality of Florensky, however, it is endearing and deeply touches the heart—because it is *real*.

5. VISITS TO MONASTERIES; OPTINA

"I am sick of 'culturedness' and sophistication," Florensky said. "I want simplicity."[9] He accepted Orthodoxy just as it was, and he shared in the direct, "grassroots" faith of the "masses." Other religious philosophers, such as Nicholas Berdyaev (who has unforunately become more well-known in the West), wanted Orthodoxy on their own terms, playing with it and modifying it to make it somehow "worthy" of their inflated estimation of themselves and of their "higher" understanding. They had a theoretical regard and admiration for the simple people who composed the heart of Russia, but they were not amidst them, not a part of them and their faith; and thus they deprived themselves of genuine spirituality. About Berdyaev and other people of "the new religious understanding," Florensky wrote: ". . . They cease to see what is in front of their eyes, which is given to them, and which they do not know and do not understand inwardly; in pursuing everything they are deprived of that which is. . . . If only for a short time a calm sobriety would return to them, then perhaps they would see—these people of false understanding—that they have no solid ground under their feet and that they are speaking sterile words, words which they themselves are beginning to believe."[10]

A telling incident, which occurred at the time of Florensky's soul-searching in 1910, illustrates the disparity between

9. *Ibid.*, p. 71.

10. P. A. Florensky, *Stopl i Utverzhdenie Istiny (The Pillar and Foundation of Truth)* (Moscow, 1914), pp. 128-129.

Check my translation

Florensky and the religious intelligentsia with which he was associated in his work. Berdyaev, with an air of dilettantism typical of the intelligentsia, said that he wanted to make an "experiment" of a trip to the Zosima Hermitage to meet with the Elders. One of the Elders there at the time happened to be Schema-Abbot Herman, a former disciple of Elder Isidore. Elder Herman was a deeply spiritual man who had acquired prayer of the heart and had written a valuable book on the Jesus Prayer.[11] Florensky knew the Elder's stature, though outwardly the Elder was just a simple peasant.[12]

Berdyaev's friend, Novoselov, attempted to bring along many of the intelligentsia to take part in the "experiment." Florensky agreed to go, although, as it turned out later, he had wanted to go by himself, without so many intruders. For many of the others, going to see an Elder was like a novelty, like going to the zoo. For Florensky, it was a matter of life and death, a question of the soul's salvation.

Remembering his trip to the hermitage, Berdyaev wrote: "I went there together with Novoselov and Sergius Bulgakov. . . . In church, behind me stood P. A. Florensky, then not a priest yet. I looked back and saw that he was weeping. They told me later that he was going through a very difficult time." That night Florensky ran away, evidently with the intention of returning sometime without the others. As for Berdyaev, he was too full of himself to perceive the secret of divine wisdom, clothed in simple garb, without sophistication or fancy rhetoric. About the great Elder Herman, he only had these patronizing words to say: "He was a simple *muzhik,* without any education. However, he did leave an impression of being quite kind and benevolent.[13]

11. Schema-Abbot Herman, *Zaveti o Delanie Molitvennom (Testament on the Activity of Prayer)* (Platina, California: St. Herman Press, 1984).

12. Florensky mentions Schema-Abbot Herman, calling him a "holy Elder," on p. 128 of the present book.

13. Nicholas Berdyaev, *Self-Awareness* (Paris: YMCA Press, 1983), pp. 214-215.

At about the time of this trip to Zosima Hermitage, Florensky planned to accompany Bishop Anthony on a pilgrimage to Solovki Monastery in the far north of Russia. This was prevented by his marriage to a humble girl named Maria, the sister of his roommate. He was, however, able to make several pilgrimages to a monastery closer to Moscow: the great Optina, which kept alive the Orthodox tradition of eldership, disseminated patristic books and was largely responsible for the spiritual blossoming in 19th century Russia. At Optina, Florensky came under the guidance of Elder Anatole the Younger, who in turn sent Florensky and his other spiritual children to Archpriest Aleksei Mechiev,[14] a saintly man who was in the Optina "lineage" and had a parish in Moscow. Florensky developed a close bond with both Fr. Anatole and Fr. Aleksei, and after the latter's death he wrote a eulogy filled with profound insights.[15]

6. THE PILLAR AND FOUNDATION OF TRUTH

In 1911, a year before his marriage, Florensky was ordained to the priesthood by Bishop Theodore Pozdeyev. While undertaking his pastoral and teaching duties, he defended his master's thesis *Of Spiritual Truth*, which was later to be amplified into the more lengthy *Pillar and Foundation of Truth*, Florensky's *magnum opus*. This highly original work, which he dedicated to the Church, combined his knowledge of theology, patristics, mathematics, science, medicine, history, linguistics and art. Filled with poetic inspiration, it deals with complex subject matter in simple, clear language, in Florensky's personal style. It is composed of twelve chapters with titles such as "Doubt," "Light of Truth," "The Comforter," "Contradiction," "Sin" and "Friendship." Each chapter, in accordance

14. See *The Orthodox Word* (Platina, California), no. 132 (1987).
15. *Otets Aleksei Mechiev* (Paris: YMCA Press, 1970).

with Florensky's experiential, personal approach to philosophy, is intended as a "letter" to a friend.

From the first published edition of *The Pillar and Foundation of Truth,* Bishop Theodore Pozdeyev ommitted the letter on "Sophia," and then upheld the Orthodoxy of the remaining text. Although the ommitted letter was included in subsequent editions, Bishop Theodore Pozdeyev's initial decision was probably for the best. Florensky, possibly in an attempt to formulate a conceptual basis for his experience as a boy of the wisdom of God in nature, made statements in the "Sophia" chapter which—although explicitly *not* pantheistic—could lead the undiscerning to ideas approaching pantheism.

Too much emphasis has been placed on Florensky's "sophiology" in the context of his whole life's work, both by his detractors and his admirers. We have mentioned it here only because he is often wrongly dismissed on the grounds of this one facet of his earlier writings. In discussing "sophiology" in connection with Florensky, it is important to bear in mind two things. First, it was Fr. Sergius Bulgakov, not Florensky, who attempted to create a complete theological system based on the Wisdom of God, or "Sophia," as constituting a kind of personal "World-Soul." Florensky only offered various sketchy speculations, drawing on what was already *there,* in Orthodox theology, iconography and liturgical traditions, leaving many questions unanswered. He realized that some of what he wrote in *The Pillar and Foundation of Truth* was "almost undemonstrable." "It is for just this reason," he stated to the "friend" to whom he addressed this book, "that I am writing 'letters' to you instead of composing an 'article.' I fear the making of assertions and prefer to question."[16]

Another thing to remember is that, after the publication of *The Pillar and Foundation of Truth,* Florensky of his own accord changed some of his earlier conceptions which were potentially dangerous to the purity of the Church's teaching, and

16. P. A. Florensky, *op. cit.,* p. 129.

moved away from his original "sophiology."[17] Later in life, when he was asked about his book as a whole, he replied, "Oh, I grew out of that!"[18] This, of course, is not to say that the book is then to be dismissed as a mere juvenile attempt, but rather that Florensky's mature philosophy should not be judged solely on the basis of this book's merits or shortcomings.

Not many years before his death, Florensky looked back on the investigations which had once found a tentative, unfinalized expression in *The Pillar and Foundation of Truth*. He saw his probings into diverse disciplines—science, theology, etc.—as an attempt to understand a single Reality from all different points of observation. "What did I do all my life?" he asked. "I investigated the world as a whole, as one picture and one reality. But I did this investigation at each given moment, or more precisely at each step of my life, from a particular angle of vision. I would investigate the relationships of the world by dissecting it in a particular direction, on a particular plane, and would strive to understand the make-up of the world from this plane which interested me. The planes were different, but one did not deny another—one only enriched the other. This resulted in a perpetual dialectic of thought, 'the exchange of planes of observation,' while at the same time viewing the world as one."[19]

In this statement can be found the essence of Florensky's relevance for modern man. In our age, when all truths are seen as relative and knowledge is fragmented into specialized compartments, it takes a unique man like Florensky to master the various disciplines and tie their discoveries together within the framework of one coherent world-view. Florensky's search for

17. Robert Slesinski, *Pavel Florensky: A Metaphysics of Love* (New York: St. Vladimir's Seminary Press, 1984), p. 12.

18. From the personal reminiscences of Fr. Victor Ilienko (1892–), a former student of Florensky at the Moscow Theological Academy.

19. Letter from the Solovki concentration camp, February 21, 1937.

a single world-outlook as absolute Truth led him first to religion in general and finally to the Orthodox Church. It was there that he found the "pillar and foundation of Truth," and this foundation gave absolute significance to his investigation of relative things—for all things now had one unchanging point of reference. He came to be considered a "religious thinker" only because he was an honest and fervent man who would be satisfied with nothing less than wholeness and completeness in his philosophic vision.

7. THE CHURCH

Although Florensky is remembered in secular circles as a scientist and in church circles as a philosopher, it was neither science nor theology that, in the end, became the center of his life, but his priesthood. His retiring yet powerful personality, imbued with a mystical timbre, helped bring many to faith in Christ. When he served the Liturgy, he did so very peacefully, pronouncing every word clearly and not loudly. He was a "celebrant of the Divine," calling down grace from Heaven and being in awe before the mystery enacted in the Eucharist. He totally immersed himself in the church services, knowing that it is the direct encounter of Life in the Church, rather than abstract reasoning, that brings one to the Truth. "Orthodoxy," he once said, "manifests itself; it does not prove itself." And he found that manifestation in the worship of the Church.

Florensky believed that the criterion of what was genuinely "churchly" could not be merely conceptual, lying outside the experience of human life. It could not be the juridical criterion of Roman Catholicism, with its emphasis on heirarchy and legality, nor could it be the scientific *Sola Scriptura* criterion of Protestantism, which Florensky found to be also conceptual and therefore open to misuse. For Florensky, the surest criterion of the authenticity of life in the Church was what he called *spiritual Beauty*. We have already encountered this idea in connection with what Florensky said about ascetics. He saw this beauty in Elder Isidore, about whom he said: "He listened to God's creation, and God's creation listened to him. Invisible threads united him with the hidden heart of creation. Not only was the world a sign for Elder Isidore, but the Elder himself was a sign for the world."

Thus, spiritual beauty manifests itself when one is united with all creation by being united in love with its Creator. This loving union both constitutes and is made possible by life in Christ's Church. Without it, Florensky felt, temporal and even eternal existence is meaningless. "I want real love," he wrote. "I understand life only as union; without this 'union' I do not even want salvation. I am not rebelling, not protesting. I simply do not have a taste for life nor for the salvation of my soul, as long as I am alone."[20] In another place he stated: "Without love—and for love it is necessary in the first instance to love God—without love the personality is broken up into a multiplicity of fragmentary psychological moments and elements. The love of God is that which holds the personality together."[21]

"Orthodox" literally means "right glorification." In Florensky's view, however, being "right" may have nothing at all to do with being Orthodox or being in the Church. A person may take precautions to be perfectly "right" merely out of insecurity, while faith in Christ remains lacking. In essence, being Orthodox actually means saving one's soul and changing one's heart, making use of the "right" forms in order to assist in this. It does not mean being right. As Florensky stated: "Half-belief, which is afraid of falling into unbelief, fearfully clings to the forms of religious life. Not capable of seeing in them the crystallized realities of Spirit and Truth, it evaluates them as juridical norms of law. It has an external attitude towards them, and values them not as windows to the light of Christ,

20. "Iz Vstrech s P. A. Florenskim," p. 73.
21. Lossky, *op. cit.*, p. 186.

but as the conditional requirements of external authority. The Christian consciousness, however, knows that the established ways of the Church are not accidental, and are offered by her as favorable conditions for salvation."[22]

8. CONFESSING THE FAITH

In the years preceding the Russian Revolution, Florensky's enormous creative energies continued to be diffused into a number of areas. Although he liked to keep to himself, he nevertheless became the leader of various organizations and brotherhoods which promoted spiritual interests. From 1911 to 1917, he edited a theological journal, writing several articles for it. He kept in contact with many outstanding Orthodox thinkers of the time: Fr. Valentin Sventitsky,[23] Fr. Sergius Mechiev (the son of Archpriest Aleksei) and others. Not abandoning his other pursuits, he did research and had treatises published in the fields of mathematics, applied science and linguistics.

The Moscow Theological Academy was closed after the Russian Revolution, and Florensky was forced to take a different course in life. He now found work in official scientific posts, lecturing on the theory of perspective at a technical-artistic school and serving as one of the chief electrical engineers for his country. Several important scientific discoveries were made by him, including the invention of a famous non-coagulating machine oil. In published essays he anticipated the development of cybernetics; and one of his works, *The Doctrine of Dielectrics,* became a standard textbook.

With the Revolution, Optina Monastery became State property, and the Soviet authorities began to persecute the monks there. Elder Anatole, having been tortured and mocked, provi-

22. P. A. Florensky, "Christianity and Culture," in *Journal of the Moscow Patriarchate,* 1983, no. 4.

23. See *The Orthodox Word* no. 111 (1983).

dentially died on the night before he was to be arrested and taken away. The other Optina Elder of that time, Elder Nektary,[24] was sent to the village of Kholmishcha, from where he was in contact with Florensky and gave him spiritual guidance. This contact continued until the Elder's death in 1928.

During the years 1925-1927, the Soviets finally closed Optina, attempting at the same time to keep their bloody deeds hidden. Demonstrating his great love for this monastery and what it represented, Florensky boldly issued an urgent appeal entitled "Save Optina!"—which of course won him no favor in the eyes of the authorities.

Although many of his former activities were repressed under the yoke of the atheist regime, it was this very yoke that enabled him to reveal his full stature as a man. The freedom of spirit which had been inculcated in him through Fr. Isidore and other Elders now came to the fore, and he became a confessor for the Faith.

The Soviet authorities for whom Florensky worked, seeing his value as an extraordinary research scientist, wanted him to renounce his priesthood. Not only did he not comply, but he was daring enough to wear his priest's cassock, pectoral cross and hat while working in an official capacity as a scientist, even going to the Supreme Soviet for National Economy dressed as a priest. Fearlessly walking in with his shining cross hanging from his neck, he delivered lectures to groups of Soviet scholars and old professors. This evoked the wrath of the authorities, who feared that the young Soviet students might be influenced by the "scholarly *pop*" (a derogatory term for a priest), as they called him.

Several times the Soviets imprisoned Florensky, only to find him still unyielding to their demands that he renounce his priesthood. While this helped bring about his final incarceration, the major reason was undoubtedly his open and vigorous protest against the official church policy of the Moscow Met-

24. See *Ibid.*, no. 129 (1986).

ropolitan, Sergius Starogorodsky. In this Metropolitan, the Soviets had found a "yes-man" who was willing to submit the
Church to the control of the atheist regime and deny the martyrdom of millions of Christians. Sergius even issued a declara-
tion in 1927, in which he stated that the joys and sorrows of
the Soviet regime were those of the Russian Church. To Florensky, it was abundantly clear that this was an act of false-
hood. His whole nature reacted against it. God cannot be served, he understood, on the basis of a lie. As a leading anti-Sergi-
anist spokesman who was known throughout Russia, Florensky had to be silenced.

9. EXILE AND MARTYRDOM

In 1933, Florensky was condemned to ten years of servi-
tude in a concentration camp. Of his remaining years, very little is known. Evidently he was first sent to a camp in Siberia
where, still refusing to deny his Faith, he was sent to a yet
worse camp on the island of Solovki. Before the Revolution,
this camp had been a thriving monastery—the very Solovki to
which Florensky had desired to make a pilgrimage as a young
man. Now there as a prisoner, he must have thought back to
his earlier aspiration of being a monk, which he now fulfilled
in a different way, being cut off from the world and suffering
for Christ in a monastery-turned-concentration camp.

In his book *The Gulag Archipelago*, Alexander Solzhenitsyn
laments the imprisonment, persecution and death of Florensky
in the camps, stating that Florensky was "perhaps one of the
most remarkable men devoured by the Archipelago of all
time." According to Solzhenitsyn, Florensky was probably
sent last to a camp in the region of Kolyma, where "he studied
flora and minerals (in addition to his work with a pick)."[25]

What enabled Fr. Paul to persevere through those long years

25. Alexander Solzhenitsyn, *The Gulag Archipelago Two* (New York:
Harper and Row, 1975), p. 670-671.

of exile and intense hardship? The answer can come only from his own words: "Through Christ we can attain realization, on Him we can build, with Him we can become complete, by means of Him we can live. . . ."[26]

According to official information, Florensky died in exile on December 15, 1943. One cannot help noticing that he died during the same year that he was expected to be released. We can only guess whether he was deliberately killed or whether he died in the inhuman conditions of the camps.

As one who died for standing up for his Faith, Florensky was listed with the Russian New Martyrs and Confessors who were canonized in 1981. His name is to be found on the icon of the New Martyrs which was used in the glorification service.

Thus, for all Orthodox Christians who, like Fr. Paul himself, are free before God and are not hindered by political fears, he is SAINT PAUL FLORENSKY.

10. *SALT OF THE EARTH*

Florensky's singular work, *Salt of the Earth,* shows that he, unlike Berdyaev, Nicholas Lossky, Bulgakov and others of the Russian religious intelligentsia, understood that the heart of Orthodoxy was to be found in the simple, unsophisticated *muzhik* ascetics who had been touched by God. *Salt of the Earth* is not a standard Life of a Saint, any more than Florensky is a standard ecclesiastical figure. It is more of a literary "photograph" or "motion picture" of a Saint who otherwise would have gone unnoticed. As such, it is of inestimable value to people of modern times who are seeking to enter into the timeless spirit of Orthodox Christianity. The context of Elder Isidore's life has been taken away, and indeed the Elder lived on the very eve of its disappearance. Since we are now outside the Orthodox atmosphere which once nurtured Saints, stan-

26. P. A. Florensky, "Spiritism as Anti-Christianity," in *Novie Put,* 1904, no. 3, p. 155.

dard hagiographical texts—composed *within* that atmosphere— often have very little to say to contemporary Christians, and thus the models of sanctity they depict do not have much effect on and do not influence new generations. Florensky's "literary photograph," on the other hand, helps the modern person to enter *into* that atmosphere, to see the Saint as Florensky himself sees him and to respond in a direct, personal way. After reading the heart-warming narrative of a loving spiritual son as he describes the daily trifles of Elder Isidore, one feels that one *knows* the Elder, that he is already a dear friend.

How was Florensky able to achieve this *tour de force* of modern hagiography, making *Salt of the Earth* a spiritual classic on par with *The Way of a Pilgrim?* He did this by combining two seemingly irreconcilable approaches to his subject: the way of science and the way of the heart.

As we have seen, Florensky was a modern man who was thoroughly abreast with the science of his day. As a scientist with an analytical approach, he knew that one had to make accurate observations and not distort the facts according to one's opinions. When one begins arbitrarily changing numbers in a mathematical equation, the answer will invariably be wrong. When describing Elder Isidore, therefore, Florensky retained the eye of a scientist, preserving the Saint's image undistorted. With Saints as with science, Florensky endeavored to leave things as they were, in order to let the truth come out.

It is often through the reality of everyday trifles that we catch glimpses of a higher Reality. That is why Florensky cherished the whole of Elder Isidore, everything about him, even the little details of his cabin. Through keen observations and psychological hints, Florensky was able to indicate outward signs of the ascetic's inward activity, which was of course impossible to fully describe in words.

According to his same principle of leaving a thing as it is in truth, Florensky—even before the Revolution—did not want Sacred History taught in public schools. He wanted everyone to have the chance of an individual, independent conversion to

Christ, on their own volition and under no compulsion, even stumbling on their way as they learn from experience what Christianity actually is, as Florensky himself had done. Forcing religion on children in schools, he said, creates *bezbozhniki* (godless ones).

Florensky's other approach in writing *Salt of the Earth*—that of the heart—is felt on every page, so there is little need to discuss it. It is of interest to point out, however, that whenever Florensky spoke of the heart, he did not speak figuratively, but literally. In *The Pillar and Foundation of Truth,* he quoted P. D. Yurkevitch in supporting his claim that, in spiritual literature, the heart is not an allegory: "The simple reading of holy texts—if we will only not misinterpret them according to prejudicial ideas—convinces us directly that the Holy Scripture precisely and with full consciousness accepted the heart as the center of all human phenomena, both of bodily and spiritual life. . . . The sacred writers knew about the exalted significance of the head in the spiritual life of a man; nevertheless, we repeat, they saw the center of this life to be in the heart. The head was for them the apparent height of that life which is originally and directly rooted in the heart."[27]

The power of Florensky's writings lies in the fact that he speaks out of the experience of the heart, and reaches others on the elemental level of that experience.

11. PROPHECIES

Finally, a word should be said about the prophetic aspects of *Salt of the Earth.*

Many of the Russian ascetics of the 18th and 19th centuries prophesied what was to happen at the beginning of our own century, when Christianity would be persecuted and the Church in Russia would have to go into hiding. They saw that—even in their own day—church people had fallen for love

27. *Stopl i Utverzhdenie Istiny,* p. 268.

of the external, and thus the Church would have to be purged and purified through suffering. These ascetics—whether hidden away in monasteries or pursuing a path of Christian struggle in the world—preserved the ancient Orthodox *blagochestia* (piety or active spiritual life). They were *the salt of the earth* (Matt. 5:13), and thus they could perceive the *savor* of authentic Christianity departing in an undetectable way. Isidore was one of them, one of the last "deposits" of this salt, and he too warned of the coming catastrophe. Over a decade before the devastating Russian Revolution and the advent of the Soviet regime, which produced more martyrs than the whole early period of Christian martyrdom, Florensky recorded these words of Fr. Isidore: "The time of Antichrist is quickly approaching. Christians will soon be so persecuted that they will have to go into hiding."

Towards the end of *Salt of the Earth*, Florensky hints at something else that is both prophetic and apocalyptic. He quotes a portion of a Bishop's sermon at Fr. Isidore's funeral: "We don't have real monasticism at present. It still has to be founded. Fr. Isidore was a forerunner of the monasticism which is yet to come, and which began in the far-off Thebaid.'

Taken at face value, the Bishop's statement was simply not true. Florensky, who was well aware of worldliness and fakery in contemporary monastic institutions, had also seen and valued the high spiritual calibre of such monasteries as Optina, and so would never have subscribed to the idea that "real monasticism still has to be founded." He did, however, obviously see a grain of truth in the Bishop's words, or else he would not have included them out of all others. Judging from his last chapter, that truth is this: Isidore represented the only type of monasticism that can survive the deceptions and tribulations of the end times. It is the monasticism of the future.

But of what does this monasticism consist? Drawing from an ancient prophecy of St. Niphon of Constantia, Florensky indicates that it consists of *separation* from the ways of the world, and a humble willingness to be *concealed* and *hidden*.

With what but this can one stand up to persecution while remaining true to one's conscience? Florensky points out that Isidore not only concealed himself from the world, but from church people as well. He did not want to be recognized by anyone, and was for the most part ignored because he could not fit into the categories of worldly thinking. As Florensky realized, a monastery or any other ecclesiastical institution that seeks recognition, respect or credibility will be bound to betray Christ when the trials come. In contrast to this he presented us with Isidore, who, in his utter simplicity, unpretentiousness, humility and unconquerable freedom of spirit, possessed the very virtues which will enable "the monk of the future," and indeed every Christian, to remain true to Christ in whatever circumstances he is placed.

Silhouette of St. Paul Florensky by N. R. Simonovich-Efimov, 1920.

Icon of St. Paul Florensky by Mother Nadezhda Russell, 1987.

Florensky in 1909, a year before his ordination.

View of Holy Trinity—St. Sergius Monastery, near the
Moscow Theological Academy and Gethsemane Hermitage.

Florensky with F. D. Samarin.

Florensky in 1932, a year before his final incarceration.

СОЛЬ ЗЕМЛИ

ТО ЕСТЬ

СКАЗАНІЕ О ЖИЗНИ СТАРЦА ГЕѲСИМАНСКАГО СКИТА

ІЕРОМОНАХА АВВЫ ИСИДОРА

СОБРАННОЕ И ПО ПОРЯДКУ ИЗЛОЖЕННОЕ

НЕДОСТОЙНЫМЪ СЫНОМЪ ЕГО ДУХОВНЫМЪ

Павломъ Флоренскимъ

Сергіевъ Посадъ.
Типографія Св.-Тр. Сергіевой Лавры.
1908.

The cover of the original Russian edition
of *Salt of the Earth*.

Salt of the Earth

A Prologue to our brother, the devout reader

Father Isidore is no longer with us. He's no longer here. He blossomed like a flower, and how depressing it is now that this flower has faded away. He shone as bright as a small clear sun and now that light has died out. He was a rock of faith—where is our support? Everything about him caused one to marvel—his love, meekness and modesty; his impartiality, straightforwardness and independence; his unpretentiousness, selflessness and poverty; his clarity, peacefulness and spiritual comportment; and finally, his prayer. But most amazing of all was his detachment from the world. He was in the world—yet not of it; he was with people—yet not as a man. He was intimidated by nothing and no one, as he himself was above it all—and all earthly concerns fell away before his quiet smile. One glance of his could destroy all human conventions, because he was above the world and enjoyed the highest spiritual freedom. It seemed as if he didn't walk upon the earth, but was rather suspended by invisible threads to some other land. All of this filled him with an inner lightness. All those who would come to him heavily burdened would lose their heaviness. With a light smile, as if playing, he could, with impunity, turn any human conditions of common life into joy. He would venture to rise above the letter of the law, and would do so with such clarity that these actions were always memorable. The ordinary and the everyday were not simply that for Fr. Isidore. No—from the everyday and the ordinary stretched long roots to other worlds, to the "New Earth."

And now, in thought and heart, bearing witness to that "which our eyes saw and our hands felt," you shall be involuntarily drawn deeper and deeper into the life of Fr. Isidore. The significance of this life becomes more apparent, and thus the task of writing it becomes more difficult. Words don't suffice to describe that refined fragrance of spirituality which like a cloud always followed Fr. Isidore, all the more because it is very difficult to talk about the Elder in an outer way. Indeed, his outer life was very plain—in it there were no excessive occupations with outer things or fancy words.

Forgive me, then, gracious reader, for this clumsy attempt I have undertaken; and if Fr. Isidore doesn't appear to you to be more of an angel from heaven than a man of earth, then place the blame not on the honorable Elder, but on the clumsiness of the compiler of this narrative. You feel something, it seems —you're at the point of coming to grips with the truth about Fr. Isidore. But writing can never do justice to what Fr. Isidore was really like.

CHAPTER 1

in which the devout reader is informed about Fr. Isidore's cell.

In order for you to know how Fr. Isidore lives, truth-loving reader, let's go together to visit his place. First we leave the Monastery of St. Sergius of Radonezh, pass by Sergiev Posad[1] and then cross through the field, which is near the *skete's*[2] ponds. Then, having crossed a little bridge and gone through the woods, we find ourselves situated between two sketes—Gethsemane and that of Chernigov. However, before really heading to the Elder's place, we must not forget to pray in the underground church of Our Lady of Chernigov, the miraculous sacred treasure in this locality. Indeed, the Elder loves this place so much that he is sure to ask us, as he indeed asks each of his guests, whether or not we have been there.

Let's proceed without further ado to the Gethsemane Hermitage. We'll now climb the wooden staircase and pass by the churchyard. Then Fr. Isidore's little house will come into view.

The little house in which Fr. Isidore lived twice,[3] and in

1. Or Şergiev Village, a city on the outskirts of Moscow, named after St. Sergius of Radonezh and the monastery dedicated to him. It was later called Zagorsk by the Soviets.

2. *Skete*: a hermitage or small monastery.

3. Both before and after he lived at the Skete of the Paraclete. *(Author's note)*

which he died, is situated at a right angle from the main entrance of the hermitage, at the very wall itself. Earlier, this little house belonged to the Mount Athos Elder Samuel, Hieromonk Ioannicius, and then to Fr. Abraham, who before that time had spent many years underground in the so-called "caves" adjoining the underground church of Our Lady of Chernigov. Fr. Isidore's house is a small hut made of logs, and consists of a little cell with a few small benches which can barely accomodate 4-5 people; an "entrance hall" (as Fr. Isidore would call it), in which only two people, at most, can be seated; and a front room. Besides this, adjoining the entrance hall is a storage room (in which Fr. Isidore has placed the samovar[4]). Both the front room and the storage room are quite small; the samovar takes up all the space in the tiny storage room and only two persons can make their way through the front room at any one time, as long as they aren't too big. During the last two years of Fr. Isidore's life, another small front room was built adjoining the house—yet it was barely big enough for two people.

This tiny toy-like house contains many nooks and crannies. As you enter it, you somehow begin to remember things —even though it's impossible to remember everything—as some half-forgotten, dear, sweet dream of the heart. Everything is extremely simple and poor, yet special, with a warm appearance, and quiet. Things have their own eyes; and Fr. Isidore's interior meets the sight so cheerfully and invitingly, and bids farewell with such endearing glances. As you enter—straight at you look the holy icons. Each has its own story and is connected with some important personage: important, however, not here on earth, but in the Kingdom of Heaven. Below the icons is a shelf containing a Jerusalem cross, decorated with pearls; an old ragged copy of the Gospels, in a shabby and glossy leather binding; and an icon-lamp on a blue glass table. All the walls of the cell are adorned with picture postcards

4. Samovar: an urn used to heat water for tea.

from all different people tied spiritually to Fr. Isidore; pictures, poems and candy wrappers. All of this may seem insignificant, but with Fr. Isidore everything had a reason for being. Everything was a symbol of the heavenly and reminded one of the highest. As the most worthy Abbot of Mt. Sinai, St. John Climacus, said: Those who love God are characteristically moved to joy and God-like love, as well as by both secular and spiritual songs, whereas just the opposite is true for those prone to voluptuousness.

One thinks that a real painting hanging on Fr. Isidore's walls, rather than these simple pictures, would have made his little cell lose its gentle character: God loves humility, and in poverty is He made strong.

So, you have entered into the cell. To the right of the icons is a window, below which is a small table with scattered books, letters and papers. Then, to the left of the icons is a little bench and a small table, on which are lying a rather tattered *epitrachelion,*[5] vestment cuffs with ragged edges, sundry items and a small shelf. Above the little table there are two little windows. On the window ledges there are "flowers," as Father would call them; cans with moss in them— tin cans with some kind of weeds well tended to by the gardener; a corked bottle filled with water in order to serve as a vessel for any "flower"; a bottle with a broken willow branch. . . . It's hard to recall everything that was on the window sill at Fr. Isidore's.

In the entrance hall stands a small cupboard filled with dishes, as well as a little table on which tea was served. There are also wooden hangers made from knotty wooden sticks— quite like antlers—and Fr. Isidore would have to show them to each of his visitors.

Passing through the front room, you enter into a small garden, measuring not more than two arshins[6] wide. The

5. *Epitrachelion:* a stole worn by Orthodox clergy.
6. About 5 feet.

garden is spread out between the skete wall and the little house, skirting the house and enclosing it on both sides by a tall plank fence with a garden gate. This so-called "Inner Desert" is where Fr. Isidore would retire for prayer and spiritual contemplation. Tall willow trees grow above the "Inner Desert," and sometimes the entire "Desert" becomes whitened with their flying fluff. But Father, with childlike joy, and glancing all around, would say, "It looks as if it's been snowing here!" The "Desert" also contained herbs tended to by the gardener, nettles and onions: some in tin cans kept dusted by the Elder himself, others planted straight in the earth. Toads and all types of living creatures also live here in Fr. Isidore's "Desert." There is also a little table made on a stump of wood, and another stump for sitting, as well as additional seating being provided by stones which the master of the "Desert" has picked up from various places. But everything your eyes see here has its own symbolic meaning: the willow—this is the Oak of Mamre, under which the Forefather Abraham received the Holy Trinity; the stone benches represent the cliffs of the Thebaid; the branching twigs which are joined together by a wooden cross and nailed to the tree (right across from the garden gate, in the corner of the "Desert") and which remind one of antlers—as the Elder himself said—represent a vision of St. Eustathius Placidas.[7] In this "Desert" there is not a single corner without its own special meaning. Even the air itself is filled with memories of the lives of the Forefathers and Saints. For Fr. Isidore, events of sacred Scripture and Church history are much closer, clearer, and more alive than the commotion of the world.

If we open the gate, we leave the "Inner Desert" and enter the "Outer Desert," which lies just in front of the little house. This is not an enclosed spot, but is only a bit protected by

7. St. Eustathius saw a cross between the antlers of a deer. See his life in "The Orthodox Word," Vol. 7, no. 1 (36), 1971.

trees and bushes. Here, under the shade of trees, a round table is rooted to the ground and around it is "furniture," as Fr. Isidore would say: that is, a "divan," an "armchair," a "chair," and so on—made of crooked twigs and boards. Fr. Isidore himself assembled this furniture. It's difficult to imagine anything more awkward looking.

In the summer time, Father would often serve tea in this "Outer Desert." He would sometimes lead his guests to the "furniture" and then inform them with a smile, "I too have a divan. It's very nice to stretch out and relax. I often relax here. It's very nice." "Here, *Batiushka,*[8] why don't you lie down here for awhile?" he would sometimes address a Bishop. How pleasant it is to sit down on these twigs, a few of which manage to poke into your side with their sharp points! Around the "furniture" were situated several small garden beds: two with vegetables and one with strawberries. A currant bush even sprouted up here.

8. *Batiushka:* an endearing term for "Father."

CHAPTER 2

in which we are told how the Elder would greet the devout reader, if the latter were to visit the Elder—and when it was appropriate to venerate the sacred objects of the Gethsemane Skete.

So now we have seen all of Fr. Isidore's dominion. Let's go now to pay him a visit, patient reader. He receives all of his guests affectionately—be they untimely or timely— and he even greets strangers as someone close, someone he has known for a long time, one of his own relations. Perhaps you don't believe it, dear reader, but it's true that everyone is close and dear to him; everyone is a father, mother, brother and sister to him, and even more.

Let's go up to the door. If the key is still sticking out of the door, this means that the Elder is home. Besides, it's rare that he isn't home; yet if he isn't there, then he is sure to return soon. Indeed, he only leaves to go to church for services and, very rarely, to the village, as well as to visit the Bishop at the Academy, or to see some of his other spiritual children. But, to our delight, the key is sticking out of the keyhole— which means that the master of the house is in. We knock on the door a bit timidly. The door is not opened. He most likely didn't hear our knock—he hears quite poorly. But then again—perhaps he already has somebody with him, either for confession or for a little private talk. We knock a little harder now. So it is—he didn't heed the knock—perhaps because he was immersed in prayer. But we can now hear him coming to

48

the door, walking at an old man's gait. He opens it. Never does
he ask who is at the door; he receives everyone and, although
this has at times caused him a few annoyances, he doesn't
want to disturb the established order of things. He comes out
in a white canvas cassock and a skullcap of the same material.
He occasionally greets his guests in a pair of white canvas
trousers and a similar kind of shirt worn outside the trousers.
Over his shirt he wears a *paramon;*[9] his feet, however, are
usually bare and seldom does he ever wear boots. He greets
us and bids us welcome.

We enter and take off our coats. The master shows us his
skillfully made clothes rack. We make the sign of the cross
together with him in front of the icons and ask for a blessing.
He blesses and kisses each one of us and then bids us to sit.
For some reason, we all felt that this blessing was not like
other blessings, but indeed was something special. Yet no one
could say in what way it was so special. At first, we felt that it
was due to the Elder's complete sincerity and conviction. And
that is true: the Elder was deeply convinced that a blessing is
charged with power and not merely a simple ritual. Later on,
we saw that it was the obvious, inner, selfless love the Elder
had for each one being blessed that made it so special; but this
only became apparent to each of us much later. There was
something, yet it was not something you could reason. Finally, you would just give up reasoning and simply say, "This
is the grace of God. Such power always emanates from holy
men." Having given up trying to understand everything by
reasoning, now you can totally relax again and, what is more,
it seems as if everything becomes self-evident.

Fr. Isidore would say something encouraging. If two of us
were to arrive together, then he would recall the travellers
from Emmaus; if we were three persons, that was especially
good: "And God appeared to Abraham as three travellers."

---

9. *Paramon:* a square piece of cloth, depicting a cross, which is worn
by monks.

Sometimes Fr. Isidore would cordially remark that it was us in particular whom he had been waiting for, that today a tasty morsel had deliberately been brought to him, or still yet, that God Himself had brought these guests to him, because it was necessary to ask them to fulfill some sort of mission, almost always thought up on the spot, so that the guests would cheer up. Yes! If we didn't forget to bring him a little present, then we wouldn't feel shy offering it to him: Father receives as easily as he gives, with thankfulness and joy. Indeed, he constantly has guests, and entertains them with the very little he has. A little present would come from whatever he had to give (the Elder never sent anyone away without a gift).

Now he begins to lead us around the cell. For someone visiting for the very first time, he will, without fail, begin to explain the history of several faces depicted on the picture postcards. He begins to recite some religious poetry. He then turns his attention to his flowers and sits us down to the reading of the Psalms, which were put to verse by a blind priest; or else he offers to join everyone in singing something from the book on the Rite of the Burial of the Mother of God which was served in Gethsemane Skete. He even requests that someone take the book home with him and make a copy of it in order to be able to sing it at home sometime. He would then recite something from George the Recluse and would mention Nikolai V. Gogol (Fr. Isidore's brother was a valet at the home of the Counts Tolstoy and was present at Gogol's death), whom Fr. Isidore highly honored—mainly, it appears, through the increasingly widespread distribution, by Fr. Isidore, of the verses:

> O Holy Mother, pure and blessed,
> To thee I dare my voice to raise, (and so forth)

which Fr. Isidore attributed to Gogol.

Then he would leave his guests alone, while he went out to set the samovar to boil and to prepare some refreshments, with which he would wholeheartedly treat his guests. We would pray, then sit down to tea, one of us taking a seat on Fr. Isidore's bed, another on an armchair, and yet another on a little bench. During refreshments, Fr. Isidore would offer some kind of gift, teach us his Prayer of the five wounds of the Savior, express his innermost thoughts (which we'll be talking about later on), present everyone with leaflets of prayers and verses, give his blessing to all, and then bid us farewell.

CHAPTER 3

which contains a description of Fr. Isidore's refreshments.

Whenever someone comes to visit Fr. Isidore, the gray-haired monk begins hustling and bustling all around just like a youthful servant, offering both food and drinks to the guests, whomever they may be. Abba[10] is afraid that his visitors will leave without being treated. The samovar is set to boil and the food is brought out and placed on the table in the hallway. Guests who are not used to all this fuss on the part of the Elder sometimes get disturbed and try to slow him down and beg him to do less running around. Yet the Elder always refers to the example set by Abraham who, for all his hospitality, was rewarded with the Holy Trinity; and he continues running around. Nothing seemed to stop him; and anyone who would visit him on a regular basis would no longer make any attempt to try to curtail his efforts. If he were stopped again, Father would always say that not only Abraham, but God Himself could be visiting us in the form of his guests, and would once again take to bustling all about.

And may God forbid, dear reader, that you should feel shy and turn down something offered. Believe me, your refusal would cause the Elder much pain. He would then tell you that something given out of love must never be refused. In fact, those were not refreshments on the table, but manifest love. Whatever he had, in all his poverty, would be laid out

10. Abba: Father.

before his guests; and if he would think of something else to offer—he would break forth rejoicing, leap up and run after the forgotten thing. A piece of watermelon which had been brought previously by a visitor; an apple, dry bread, gingerbread, a few fruit drops—Fr. Isidore divided everything equally among his guests. He left nothing for himself, alleging that he had already eaten. But if one should ask him to share in the meal, then for fear of offending his guests by refusing, he would end up taking something for himself—providing that the guests themselves had enough.

Fr. Isidore loved to mix things together which no one would have ever dreamed of mixing. Thus, he would have a pot of his famous jam—a conglomeration of leftovers of cherries, dried figs, cranberries, raisins, kvass[11] and probably turnips. Sometimes Fr. Isidore would tell us how he would prepare this jam, and with a smile would say, "Some people don't like it, but that doesn't bother me—it's delicious." He would only serve this jam to the "selected few" (as he would jokingly put it) in whom he had confidence; but in fact, he would let anyone try it. Indeed, there were reasons for this: those unaccustomed to it could barely swallow a whole spoonful of the ascetic jam. Yet Fr. Isidore would eat several spoonfuls himself and continue praising its merits.

Even in such details as Fr. Isidore's "furniture," his "jam," and so forth, one is compelled to see the subtle yet very instructive irony on the "luxury of the world"—the Elder's detachment from the world, his other-worldliness. It was as if he were saying, "You think you impress me, a bearer of the Spirit of God, with your furniture, your various jars of jam, your worldly comforts. And I pay no attention to all your comforts, because when the Spirit is present, then my furniture and my jam are quite sufficient—but when the Spirit is not present, your furniture and jam are good for nothing."

11. Kvass: Russian rye-beer.

It seemed that the Elder would use his "furniture" and his "jam" as silent witnesses. However, it was as if this silent speech, being the very flower and nectar of foolishness-for-Christ, was outwardly quite different from him in its subtlety; yet if one had to apply the name "foolish" to this most subtle irony concerning the world, then Fr. Isidore could certainly be called a fool-for-Christ. This foolishness was inbred in him, so it seems, and therefore not one foolish trait was devised, premeditated, or contrived.

Just as with the jam, Fr. Isidore would sometimes prepare food in which he would mix lettuce, olives and anything else that pleased him. There was such a mixture of things that when Fr. Isidore tried to serve it everyone would refuse. But Father, with a tender smile, would say, "Come on, at least taste it."

Both here and in many other cases, it is impossible to distinguish his simplicity and love from his detachment to all worldly things. He turned everything upside down and in such a way that it was impossible to find one ounce of self-will or anything ostentatious. His simplicity was an irony; his irony was simplicity itself. He could change all existing conditions in order to allow them to be seen through the window of eternity; and—amazingly enough—he would do this without offending anyone. He would uproot everything in his guests; he would push each one off his pedestal of self-complacency and bring him back down to earth; he would drag each and every conceit through the mire. And (astoundingly!) it would be impossible to be indignant at this utter defeat: Fr. Isidore would look on—with childlike clarity—as if not having the slightest clue as to what he had done. He would attack from all positions, and not one ray of self-complacency, self-esteem or pride would shine from his wide-open, bright eyes. He would do it—and yet it was as if it wasn't him at all. He would attack conceit, although no one seemed to be able to understand how or with what he would do it.

It's best to compare it to a man charged with electricity: he would touch someone with his hand and that person would feel himself shaking, yet wouldn't believe his eyes. Indeed, the one who had touched him seemed by all appearances to be a simple man—and remained that way. That's Father for you: he would set off a spark, yet he himself would remain as before — in his white cassock, or in his shirt and trousers, smiling tenderly. Then you would begin to think once more: "He's simply a nice old man, and nothing more!"

However, let's get back to the story of Fr. Isidore's refreshments. Some distinguished guests once arrived at Fr. Isidore's cell and caught him at the samovar. Abba was boiling potatoes in the samovar. He invited his guests to have some tea, but the guests, if only to avoid such a refreshment, decisively declined the invitation. Then Fr. Isidore turned the samovar over, poured the water out and spilled the potatoes out on the floor. "Don't be afraid of the water—it's warm, but it won't be for long. I'll boil the potatoes later," he would inform his guests, while he himself would set the samovar to boil again, having understood the reason for his guests' previous refusal.

Once a Bishop came by to see Fr. Isidore, but Father, in one of his outfits, was digging up one of his garden beds. The Bishop smiled: "What a dandy you are. . . . How dashing!" "All right, all right, have a seat, Batiushka," said the Elder, smiling back. And so the procedure began anew.

I don't recall just how many times Fr. Isidore sat with Bishop Evdokim in the "Inner Desert." Some cups of tea had been placed on the wobbly little table in front of them and there were a few biscuits kept in a rusty old sardine can, as well as one and a half pieces of gingerbread. They got carried away in conversation and it began to rain; both host and guest took cover under the "Oak of Mamre," and under its protection they continued their talk. After the rain, Fr. Isidore gathered the tea cups and found the remainder of the biscuits floating in the tin can on the table. A few days later the same Bishop was having tea once again at Father's place. And once again the Elder brought out the tin of biscuits, offering for consumption that which remained from the previous time. "Yes, but they're all soggy," said the Bishop, a bit perplexed. "But I poured out the water and have dried out the biscuits, and now they are fine again," explained the Elder.

Here is yet another case, which has remained in my memory. Once Bishop Evdokim was walking through the woods near Bethany. Along the way he met two Bethany seminary students.

"What are you doing?" asked the Bishop.

"We're taking a walk."

"Instead of observing trees, you'd do better to observe people."

"But whom?"

"Have you heard of Fr. Isidore?"

They then started talking, and the Bishop led the two seminary students to see the Elder. Father received them, as he does all his guests, with a greeting and with love. He brought out some rye crackers, gave them some kvass to drink and then began talking. The seminarians left beaming with delight.

Yes, dear reader! You probably won't believe me when I tell you that as I write these lines tears of gratitude and emotion are welling up in my eyes at the thought of even one of these refreshments of Fr. Isidore. These slices of watermelon, biscuits or pieces of apple were not simply food: no, they always represented slices and pieces of love and affection.

The church of Gethsemane Skete, built in the 14th century.

Icon of Our Lady of Chernigov, to which the Chernigov Skete and underground church were dedicated.

Fr. Isidore in his "Outer Desert."

Fr. Isidore's cell.

Bishop Evdokim (†1935), a frequent visitor
to Fr. Isidore's "Inner Desert."

Paupers and peasants such as would visit Fr. Isidore.

CHAPTER 4

which informs the reader of the gifts which Fr. Isidore would offer to each person who would come to visit him.

If it is possible, to some degree, to call enthusiasm for doing good deeds a passion, then as far as Fr. Isidore is concerned, it could be said that he had his own passion—his only one—namely the passion of offering presents. No one would leave Father's cell without a present. He would never visit anyone without bringing a gift and would never appear anywhere with empty hands. He would always bring something with him: sometimes *prosphora*[12] or oil from the icon of Our Lady of Chernigov, sometimes a leaflet with a prayer, and sometimes an icon. Even in someone else's home he would always see to it that he could provide a treat. He would arrive to see the Bishop or someone else, for example, and bring along a turnip, a frozen apple, a jar of jam, gingerbread or other things.

Having offered the gift, he wouldn't think about its usefulness: he would show his love and therefore wouldn't be ashamed at its insignificance. Sometimes in the summer he would joyfully bring a cucumber or 10-15 raspberries from his own garden.

Even before seeing someone in person, he would try to deliver him some small gift as a token of his love. Sometimes you'd come to see him, and he would offer you some kind of gift and then send you on a mission: "Here's another little piece of gingerbread. Take it to Sergei. And here

12. *Prosphora:* leavened bread for use in the Divine Liturgy.

is some prosphora—please take it to so and so."

Once someone from the market district came to visit him after being away for the summer months. The Elder rejoiced: "So, you've come! For some time now I've been keeping these two little berries on the bush for you!" And indeed, in spite of the fact that it was autumn, two little berries were still hanging on the raspberry bush. The Elder plucked them off, placed them on a blade of grass and offered them with love.

But then he remembered that he should have already sent the turnip he had selected for His Eminence Bishop Evdokim a long time ago. He went to pull it out of the ground. Someone else who was also present offered his assistance, because the old Abba, barely walking, was pulling the turnip in vain by the leaves. But Father refused, saying, "If it's a gift, then I'll have to do it by myself." He pulled and pulled at the leaves of the turnip and tore them off while standing there looking bewildered. Then came the answer. He ran for a knife and a pail. He brought some rain water from a tub back with him in the pail, and began pouring water in a circle around the turnip in order to soften the earth. Then he dug around the turnip with the knife, pulled it up and, triumphantly, went to wash it in the tub of rain water. He washed it, wrapped it in some clean paper and passed it on to the Bishop, with the words: "Let him have a treat—it is tasty." And when the Bishop received the turnip, he kissed it and concealed it in a place of honor.

But Fr. Isidore especially loved giving gifts to those who came to visit him. He would clearly suffer while trying to figure out what he was going to offer his guest as a gift. He would inspect all his belongings and he wouldn't rest content until he came up with something suitable. And so it was— not only with laymen or spiritual leaders outside the skete, but with the brothers of the skete as well.

"I brought him supper," one novice recalled, "and each time he would give me three candies: 'Here's a little consolation for you. You brought the supper here—you labored—

and this certainly has to be paid for. It was embarrassing to take a gift."

There were many such cases, for Fr. Isidore could only console those to whom he could give a little present. In an extreme case, if he didn't have anything at all, he was prepared to give away that which he himself needed the most, provided that he could offer it as a gift.

Not long before his death, he divided up all of his belongings. But we'll be telling you about that later on.

CHAPTER 5

which explains to the reader how Fr. Isidore related lovingly to all people.

Showing love for people—the rich and the poor, the learn-ed and the simple, officials and non-officials, the righteous (if such people indeed exist) and the sinners, the Orthodox and the non-Orthodox, as well as non-Christians and even heathens—was for Fr. Isidore just as necessary as breathing. He displayed goodness on all sides—simply and naturally—without planning or reasoning, not at all aware that he was doing anything special, exceptional or unique. He would never let someone leave without telling him something edify-ing, comforting and encouraging. When he would walk by, he would without fail say something nice; if he saw a somber face, he would be certain to remove the grief. If someone needed help, Fr. Isidore would give all that he had. If this was not sufficient, he would then carefully, humbly and gently ask others. If this didn't work, he was always ready to give what he could get his hands on. And since those who needed help would always flock to Fr. Isidore's place, he never seemed to have anything. He would receive a little money from some-one—and the next day it would most likely be gone. Knowing how impossible it was for him to refuse a call for help, Fr. Isidore would receive a three ruble note and quickly have it converted into change so that there would be enough for sev-eral needy people; but sometimes he would give all the money to the first person who came along. He would often send money to all corners of Russia—to somebody languishing in prison or to some soldier sent off far away from home, etc. Often he would give away his meager meal while he himself would go hungry. "One day a poor man came by," Fr. Isidore would excuse himself, "and this man said that he hadn't had anything to eat in three days, and as proof of his words he kissed the dirty hem of my garment. Now, how could you not help this man out?"

But that's how Fr. Isidore justified his actions. Often he gave whatever he had without waiting for a request. And he was often deceived.

The authorities made him the manager of the clothes and linen store there at the skete.

"Fr. Isidore's entire life," said one of the brothers of the skete, "was founded on love and devoted to the poor. The poor, the downtrodden —whether just or unjust—would go to see Fr. Isidore, more than anyone else. No one left Fr. Isidore's place without being comforted. He gave of everything he had—like the widow in the Gospels. Once someone borrowed Fr. Isidore's boots in order to go somewhere, but he never returned them. Fr. Isidore was compelled to walk about during the winter in his slippers and socks."

—Well, who took the boots?

"Do you think he will tell?"

Having learned that Father didn't mind giving away all of his clothes, the skete authorities stopped giving him new things. Here is how one brother at the skete described it: "He had a childlike simplicity about him, as well as an un-limited love for people. There was also poverty. . . no one can deny this. How many years I have lived here and have never seen him wearing a new *riason* [outer robe]. No one can say the last time they saw Fr. Isidore in a new pair of boots; he wore whatever he was given. But he was never given the good ones, since the authorities knew that he would give them away." Really, Father didn't even have a decent riason, and when he would have to leave the skete—to go to see the

Bishop, for example, or to visit the Academy—then Father would borrow Fr. Abraham's riason. But this riason was quite old too, for Fr. Galacteon had been the first in the *Lavra*[13] to wear it and Fr. Abraham had bought it from him for ten rubles. Fr. Isidore was very close to Fr. Abraham.

In the words of Elder Abraham, "Fr. Isidore got along well with the outside world. He would always have all types of people visiting him."

All types of people—monks and priests, actors and teachers, students and seminarians, soldiers, businessmen, peasants, workers—who didn't visit him? People would come to him for financial assistance, for comfort, with perplexing questions—tired of living, fearing punishment, with heavy sins, with great joy, wishing to give something to the poor, wanting to make amends with their enemies, to arrange family matters, to heal diseases, to chase out evil spirits, —people came to him for every conceivable reason. He received each one with love and tried to satisfy them all. But he especially loved the outcasts, even the guilty. When everyone turned their backs on a man, he was the one to whom Fr. Isidore showed his love more than anyone else; it was, after all, one big family. Rumors spread as to a man's involvement in shady deals— that he had deceived many and that the police were after him. But Fr. Isidore treated him with such special care. He sent him presents; in fact, Fr. Isidore would send all that he would receive to the man. He cared for him as much as he could and would instruct others to do likewise.

This is probably why Fr. Isidore treated Jews with the same special care. Whenever someone would drop by to see Fr. Isidore, the Elder would always share news about some "poor Jews," as he called them, who were attracted to Christianity through his love. He also had some Jewish godchildren whom he cared for throughout their lives. In his cell there hung a photograph of one such Jew and his family (he was a

13. I.e., Holy Trinity-St. Sergius Lavra (*Lavra* = a large monastery).

eg only converts!

barber, as I remember), and Father would always explain to his new guests what a good man this man was, as if he was afraid that they would hurt his dear Jewish friend and say something bad about him. One of these Jews, who was subject to military conscription, failed to show up where he was supposed to report—due to the simplicity of his soul (that, at least, is how Father explained it)—but instead skipped out, for which he landed in prison. From prison he sent Father a letter filled with anguish and terrible horrors, complaining about his miserable situation and begging Fr. Isidore for prayers and money. He said that only his remembrance of Fr. Isidore and the icon which Fr. Isidore had given him as a gift prevented him from taking his own life. Fr. Isidore was worried, as if it were his own son. He sent the man whatever he had and asked those who came by for a visit to send the "dear Jewish boy" something. He also wrote him in his barely legible, old man's scrawl.

This is only one of many cases. It is difficult to remember them all and it's impossible to write down all that you do remember, for Fr. Isidore's life was filled with so much good.

Likewise, for two years before his death Father cared for a young Korean, not realizing that he would be charged with taking on a Japanese spy.[14]

He would often feed someone dinner at home for a long period of time. He fed one person the whole winter. But that person stole the Elder's alarm clock, and moreover, the Elder caught him in the act. Fr. Isidore complained to one brother, "It wouldn't have mattered at all, Mikey, only, he also took a hammer and now there's nothing left to drive nails in with." The hammer, however, was later found. But afterwards, when the Elder would be asked, "Well, Father, someone stole your alarm clock," then he, with a guilty look, would smilingly say, "Oh, he didn't steal anything,

14. During the Russian-Japanese War.

he took it," and would change the topic of conversation.

Likewise, about three years before his death, Fr. Isidore took care of a worker whose arm had been cut off by a machine. Fr. Isidore would usually call him "the armless man." He would spoonfeed this "armless man" himself, undress and dress him, give him some money, and repeatedly save him from suicide attempts. Fr. Isidore would receive some alms and, without losing any time, would hurry to give it to the "armless man." Whose assistance didn't he ask for the crippled man? Whatever the topic under discussion, Father would never fail to turn the conversation to the "armless man" and would begin to plead his case. The Elder went to a great deal of trouble on his behalf. But having to select from many similar instances, I will relate one such incident to you, dear reader. Once a student dropped by to see Fr. Isidore and saw quite a spectacle: the one-armed worker was excitedly trying to persuade Father that he, the worker, must either shoot himself or hang himself, since this apparently was the sentence passed onto him by the revolutionaries. Father then turned towards the student who had just come in and began complaining about the worker. If the "armless man" wouldn't take Fr. Isidore's words to heart, then perhaps he would listen to the student. But, of course, he didn't heed the student's attempts at persuasion either. Not having obtained any resolution for the situation, both the Elder and the student knelt down and prayed for understanding on the part of the crippled man. Then Fr. Isidore hurried off to see Elder Barnabas in order to enlist some more help; but Fr. Barnabas, probably having foreseen what it was all about, refused to take part in talks with the "armless man." Then the aged Abba Isidore, together with the "armless man," again left the monastery enclosure and headed for the student's room, which the student had checked out at the monastery's guest house. Here they once again offered the worker some tea; they tried to persuade him; they implored the man to abandon his plan. Father began inventing new and yet newer schemes. He brought some prosphora and offered it to the worker in small pieces. He then took off his own pearl cross, which had been brought to him from Old Jerusalem by some pilgrim, and, having taken it from around his neck, he placed it around the worker's neck. Then he got some money from somewhere (he himself had none of his own—as always!) and gave it to the worker, telling him that the Lord had sent this to comfort him. But the hardened heart is not wounded by love. The 80 year-old Elder then bowed down before the worker and begged him to see reason. Then the student, together with his young wife who was present at this exhortation, also bowed to the worker. And the worker bowed before the Elder. How all these requests would fare was known only to God. But outside interference put an end to them. Suddenly the janitor knocked at the door and asked the student to vacate the room, since it had been discovered that the "armless man" was politically suspect. The student had to gather all of his belongings and quickly leave the guest house. But Batiushka, standing by the gate of the skete and bidding farewell to the departing student and his wife, spoke the words of our Savior: "Blessed are they which are persecuted for righteousness' sake."

CHAPTER 6

in which the Orthodox reader is told of Fr. Isidore's God-like kindness towards all of God's creatures, to lowly beasts, to all things growing on the earth, and to everything which contains the breath of life.

Fr. Isidore was kind to all, even to the lowest of creatures. He cared not only for those who were made in the image of God, but also had compassion for the lowest of animals. In short, he cared for all living creatures. He was charitable and fed wild animals and birds; he even kept reptiles, frogs, mice and rats. Yet if the old Abba were ever ill, he never forgot his little brothers and would ask others to feed his family. Even right before his death he asked a member of his household about the cat's health. "Well," he would say, "is the cat getting better?" "Yes, it's better." "Thank God. Thank God."

Once it happened that a cat was lying on the road and snacking on some kind of little bird. It took a great deal of effort for Fr. Isidore to force the cat the let go of the wounded bird. That's how a little sparrow with a damaged wing came to live at the Elder's cell until it was healed.

Once he was asked, "Father, don't the mice ever bother you?" The Elder smiled: "No, they don't bother me at all. I feed them lunch and supper and that keeps them quiet. Before, they would claw their way all over the cell. But now I put food out for them to eat—near the mouse holes—and they don't run around anymore. No, they don't bother me at all."

"I now have a guest with me and no longer live on my own," the Elder once said to the Bishop. The Bishop had an inquisitive look on his face. "—A frog has just arrived in the 'Desert'," explained Fr. Isidore with a joyful smile. "They all seem to be running away," said the Bishop. "Yes, it ran away but has come back again. I now sing a little with it and we talk—and now it doesn't run away any more." And indeed, on one of the rocks of the Thebaid (which the attentive reader already knows about) sat a big frog. Father lowered his gray beard over the silent creature and, looking with his clear eyes directly into the eyes of the frog—and in his old man's voice, sang the Psalms of the meek King David.

Another Abba, St. Macarius the Great, repeatedly said that just as the sun shines its light on all that is unclean and the dirt therefore no longer pollutes but remains clean, likewise God's grace enters into each soul and the soul remains unblemished. An abundant force was emitted from Fr. Isidore of Gethsemane and went out to all who came near him—both man and beast; Abba would always remain "above the world."

Father had a special love for plants, grass, flowers: everything which the earth gave birth to. He would spot an uprooted weed and would take it and place it in his "Inner Desert" or in his room—in an old sardine can he had found along the road. That's how he acted, because he felt sorry for the silent and quiet children of the earth. For that same reason, he would also plant nettles in the "Desert." With the same joy he would gather up broken branches and place them in water.

The Elder would not allow others for any reason to harm one of God's creatures. "We all came together once after the evening prayer rule," related one of the brothers of the skete, "and below the Elder's window there grew a type of grass (from which vegetable cutters are made). But, without asking, we cut some off. Fr. Isidore came out and said, 'Who did this?' Another who was with me said, 'Michael cut it, but I brought it here.' 'Well, turn towards the Church of the Resurrection and pray.' The brother then went down on his knees and began to pray. Then Fr. Isidore called him to come over and gave him three pieces of candy as a treat for having spoken to him so harshly. But Fr. Isidore continued looking after the grass and watering it."

Much more could still be told to you concerning the Elder's kindness towards all creatures, dear reader. But enough has been said to attest to the fact that he truly was one who had a great feel for the earth and was a father not only to people, but to everything that breathes and lives on the earth.

CHAPTER 7

*which shows how gentle, forgiving and peaceful Fr. Isidore
was, as well as the forgiveness he showed for each offense in-
flicted on him.*

Fr. Isidore was independent and free. He was simple,
gentle, forgiving and non-judgmental. He wouldn't judge
or get angry with anyone, but would endure everything.
There was no end to his forgiveness: if he noticed that someone had been annoyed or offended by him, he would immediately ask for forgiveness, even though he wasn't guilty
of anything. If someone spoke an offensive word about him
and, despite all of Father's efforts, he still couldn't soften
the heart of the offender, then Father would quietly take
to the sidelines and wait for a more favorable opportunity.

He would also encourage others to do the same, continually serving as an example to others himself. If words
of judgement were spoken in Father's presence, then he would
gently yet firmly and decisively put a stop to them in such
a way that it was impossible to say another word. If he saw
that two people were arguing with each other or even simply
that their mutual love for each other was growing cold, he
would always encourage them to make peace with each
other and to ask for forgiveness. Mostly, he would always
encourage the one with whom he was talking, even though
that person may have been entirely in the right. Fr. Isidore
would request, beseech and finally, in a quiet and gentle
way—yet persistently and decisively—demand it, in such a

way that no one would have dared disobey the Elder.

What exactly did take place between the spiritual father and his spiritual children — only those involved know, and their Heavenly Father. Fr. Isidore didn't say a word or nod his head about this to anyone. These disclosures were forever hidden in the spiritual depths of the Elder, like a rock in the ocean deep. After the matter was finished, it was as if he would wipe it completely from his mind and memory, and would banish it from his very being. That would mean that it no longer existed and there was nothing more to talk about. But it's worth telling you, dear reader, about a few of these instances in Father's life.

Once Father housed, fed and took care of an expelled seminarian. But the seminarian proved to be ungrateful. A bad thought from the primordial enemy of the human race—the devil—entered into him: he planned to stab the Elder and rob him of all his humble possessions. One day when the master of the house was away, the seminarian began to fumble around everywhere searching for some money. Just then Fr. Isidore arrived. The seminarian, waving the knife at him, demanded, "Give me all your money!" However, there was no money in Fr. Isidore's house. Indeed, he always gave it away to the first person who requested it.

While the seminarian, with his knife in hand, continued to demand money that didn't even exist, some members of the brotherhood dropped by to pay the Elder a visit.

The Abbot reproached the Elder: "Why do you always take on these needy people?"

But the Elder excused himself, saying, "Batiushka, what can you expect of me, an old man? —God knows what. After all, this is my only consolation."

The Abbot did not do anything about Fr. Isidore and the Elder continued to take on people who sometimes behaved badly towards him. But Father carefully kept this hidden, and it became known only by sheer chance.

So what then was the outcome of all this? Here's what

happened: legal action was taken against the seminarian, but Fr. Isidore saved the villain from punishment. At the trial, as Fr. Isidore was being called to give testimony, he was asked if the seminarian had intended to stab him. But Father replied, "No, he didn't want to stab me." Now the judge, with a look of surprise, said, "Then how is it that he was waving a knife all around and crying out that he was going to stab you?"

"Yes, indeed—that's what he cried out. But anyone can cry out that they are going to stab someone."

The seminarian was informed that he was being set free on the basis of Fr. Isidore's testimony.

Here's how another such incident turned out. Fr. Isidore was once insulted in the kitchen. He had dropped by the kitchen to ask for something, but his request was rudely dismissed by the cellarer's assistant. Just think, dear reader, would Fr. Isidore be the kind of man who would ask for something personally for himself? Yet, even if he were to ask for something personal, who would dare judge him? But in this case, he was so rudely refused that it was clearly an insult. For this sin, or for some other reason, it so happened that the guilty one fell seriously ill soon after the mentioned incident, and was lying in bed, close to death. As soon as Fr. Isidore heard about this, he went to his offender and asked for forgiveness. "I might have offended you," he said, "by asking for something that wasn't really necessary." After that, the cellarer's assistant began to get better.

Fr. Isidore would not only forgive others their offenses committed against him, but would cover his brother's sins with love—as well as try to keep them hidden from everyone else. For example, there was a certain frequent visitor to Fr. Isidore's who was either a novice or a layman, dressed in novitiate clothing. Father would constantly offer him tea to drink, help him out and go to great pains for him. But this "novice" would treat Fr. Isidore badly: he would go to someone and ask for something in Father's name. It wasn't known

whether Father had sensed this or not, but one day the whole
affair came to light. One day the "novice" visited one of
Fr. Isidore's spiritual sons and asked for some envelopes,
writing paper and stamps in Fr. Isidore's name. The spiritual son then said, "Fine, I'm going to Fr. Isidore's myself
today, so I'll bring them along with me." So he arrived at
Fr. Isidore's, handed him the package and said, "Here you
are, Father. Here's what you asked for. . . ." But Father denied
it, saying, "No, I didn't ask for these." "But Brother so-and-
so just told me so." Father thought for a moment and suddenly understood that his name was being used in the wrong way,
but he wanted to conceal the brother's sin. Terribly embarrassed by this unexpected discovery, with a clear feeling of
shame for the brother, he decided not to insist that he had
not requested writing materials. "It's good that you brought
some paper . . . it will be of use sometime," he said, taking the
package and moving the topic of conversation on to something
else. In this way, he neither exposed the sinner, nor did he
judge him.

Not only did Fr. Isidore himself forgive others their offenses, but he would encourage others to do the same. To
establish peace was an absolute necessity for him. Here is
one example of this, and from this example the reader will
learn at the same time of Fr. Isidore's relationship to the
famous Elder Fr. Barnabas, who subsequently became his
spiritual son. A certain deacon who was a student at the
Theological Academy relates that he paid a visit to Father
shortly before the Elder's death. The Elder was reading the
biography of Fr. Barnabas at that time and therefore began
talking about the book, approving of it but at the same time
pointing out the inaccuracy of the story found on page 17.
Here is how Fr. Isidore related the story:

Once a soldier friend dropped by to see Fr. Barnabas,
when he was still Novice Basil. Fr. Barnabas joyfully received him and offered him his Bible as a gift, which he himself
had received as a gift from Elder Daniel. When Elder Daniel

learned of what had taken place, he called the novice to him and asked about the Bible. Yet when Fr. Barnabas spoke the whole truth, Elder Daniel became angry and ordered the novice to get out of his sight. Fr. Isidore helped him out. With deep sorrow, Fr. Barnabas came to his friend and teacher (Fr. Isidore taught Fr. Barnabas to read Church Slavonic words correctly, i.e., according to their stress) and spoke of his grief, not seeing the possibility of correcting that which had happened. But Fr. Isidore found a way. "Don't grieve," he said. "I, too, have the same Bible; take mine and give it to the soldier, who is still at the inn, and take yours back from him. Then we'll go together to the Elder to ask for forgiveness." And that's what they did. On his knees before Elder Daniel, Fr. Isidore prayed for forgiveness for his friend, who at the same time was weeping. The Elder relented after such a moving request and reconciled himself with Fr. Barnabas.

CHAPTER 8

in which the pure-hearted reader will perceive that great humility in the Holy Spirit carries great independence with it.

You will soon see that great modesty and deep humility resided in Fr. Isidore's heart, attentive reader. He seldom spoke of his own works for God, save for someone else's edification: he usually kept them hidden. He never showed off, nor spoke of himself in a way that placed himself higher than anyone else. The good he would do would be kept a secret, not only from others, but from himself as well; he would do something and immediately forget about it. In truth—in the words of our Lord and Savior Jesus Christ—his right hand didn't know what his left hand was doing. Therefore, he never thought about himself, but always considered himself as nothing, and—with absolute sincerity—was convinced that no one was worse than himself. Sometimes one's heart would leap for joy in contemplation of this heavenly beauty; sometimes the exclamation would escape from one's mouth, "Batiushka, how good you are!" But Abba, with a puzzled look on his face, would retort, "Good, you say? Why, I'm the most foolish and the least of men."

There was no pride to be found in Father. He would plead with anyone, kneel down before anyone, kiss anyone's hand— if a spiritual healing required it. He would submit himself without effort and without irritation—simply, as if selflessness were a most common affair. Yet great spiritual humility was combined with great independence in Fr. Isidore. As far as the Elder was concerned, there was not a man alive whom he felt better than, no matter how influential or high-ranking he might be. Abba said just what he thought to everyone— especially to higher authorities. And you will come to see, dear reader, that Abba feared no one. He was never ingratiating towards anyone, never forgot his human worth, always felt absolutely free and submitted himself entirely to the One God.

While still a beardless and moustacheless lay brother under Archimandrite[15] Anthony of the Lavra, he interrupted a talk between the Archimandrite and Metropolitan Philaret of Moscow. The great Hierarch and the wise Archimandrite were sitting at tea and were thinking together about all the requirements for an ecumenical council and links with the Catholics. But the question then arose as to who would take precedence at the council. It was foreseen that neither the Orthodox nor the Catholics would want to concede, and that meant the council would not take place. Then Fr. Isidore entered the room carrying a tray and teacups. "The Mother of God— that's who will be first. Therefore the presiding chair at the council meeting will remain unoccupied: it will belong to the Mother of God."

Throughout his entire life Fr. Isidore cherished the thought of uniting the Churches, and the Church divisions were a personal pain and hurt for him.

"Children of one Mother dear are we:
The suffering of our Mother we can't see,"

he sadly brought to mind while citing some poem from memory—and he would do this very, very often. It was obvious that thinking about the divisions within the Churches disturbed him very much. Sometimes he would even add, "And, after all, we are all of one system. It's all because of one letter:

15. Archimandrite: an Abbot who is in priestly rank.

we are Kafoliki[16] and they are Katoliki.[17] We must pray to
the Mother of God. Through Her shall come this unification,
for human efforts alone will not be sufficient." Father linked
the unification of the Eastern Church with the Western Church
to the final judgement of the world; and sometimes pointing
to the anti-Christian movement rising both in Russia and
abroad, he spoke his most secret, deeply nurtured thoughts:
"The time of the Antichrist is quickly approaching. Christians
will soon be so persecuted that they will have to go into hiding."

It was impossible not to believe Fr. Isidore's words. His
cloudless face would become foggy, and in an instant his
bright smile would disappear; his eyes would look serious
as they would penetrate the future. It would be frighten-
ing: something is on its way, something is on its way, something is approaching. . . . But this instant would pass—and this
prophetic seriousness would become concealed, melt slowly
away and completely disappear. However, this single instant
would be enough to put one on guard for a long time.

The thought of Church unity, in connection with these
terrible predictions, was one of Fr. Isidore's most sacred
thoughts. Once he even wrote about this to His Highness
Tsar Alexander III, William E. Gladstone and Otto Bismarck.
The letters were written in pencil, barely legible, and of
course written in Russian. Besides this, the Elder sent several prayer books to both Gladstone and Bismarck, as well as
the Prayer to the Mother of God composed by N. V. Gogol.
It is not known whether these packages and letters sent
abroad ever arrived, but it is known that the letter to His
Highness Tsar Alexander III did indeed make it to the royal
court, from where a rebuke was sent back to the hermitage.

16. "Kafoliki": epithet for the Orthodox Church; universal.

17. "Katoliki": (Roman) Catholics. For the author's own view of the
essential differences between Orthodoxy and Roman Catholicism, see
Pillar and Foundation of Truth (in Russian) pp. 58, 267, 404, 765.

Subsequently, Fr. Isidore himself spoke repeatedly of his exploit and gently smiled at the unexpected outcome of the whole affair. Yet he continued to be fearless and independent.

He even spoke of other events in his life which shed bright light upon his independence.

In the district under the abbotship of Leonid, Archimandrite of the Holy Trinity-St. Sergius Lavra, the monks were seized with fear. Leonid was formerly in the military and he brought military discipline with him into the monastery.

One instance was known, for example, in which he forced the last ascetics who had been struggling underground in caves for many years (where the present-day Our Lady of Chernigov Skete is located) to come up and eat with everyone else. "What kind of fasters are these?" said the Archimandrite.

Everything trembled before this pastor, who even in monasticism did not want to stop commanding as a colonel. From this you'll come to understand, dear reader, that Fr. Isidore— as fearless as ever—quickly came under the Archimandrite's scrutiny. The Elder was summoned and he entered into the Archimandrite's quarters. Fr. Leonid expected the Elder to come straight up to him and kiss his hand, but Fr. Isidore immediately began praying before the icons. Fr. Leonid flared up and found cause to unleash his wrath. The point is that Fr. Isidore's right arm had been a bit injured since his youth and as such he wasn't able to reach his left shoulder. Yet Fr. Leonid yelled at him, "You fool! You don't know how to cross yourself." Fr. Isidore clearly and calmly looked the Archimandrite straight in the eye and, without any challenge in his voice, simply said, "I am not afraid of you." The Archimandrite was beside himself with anger and began swearing. But Fr. Isidore again declared, "I am not afraid of you." It seems that the Archimandrite threw the Elder out the door himself. But, they say, this whole affair had a sobering effect on him, and after this he became more restrained. Father himself spoke with a smile of his clash with the Archimandrite.

Another similar situation had to do with his life in the Skete of the Paraclete. Fr. Isidore intended to build himself a storage room for trash and household refuse. But the authorities took a suspicious view of this. "Why?" they asked. "What for?" The true intention behind these questions was that the authorities wanted to cast aspersions on the Elder's character. Then came the Elder's straightforward reply: "In order to keep women here!" For giving this answer, he was banned from the Skete of the Paraclete.

Fr. Isidore's straightforwardness, his courage and independence, thoroughly protected him from all the high officials in the skete. Metropolitan Sergius of Moscow also lived there at one time, imitating Hierarch Philaret, the founder of the skete. With staff in hand, and without any formality whatsoever, he would sometimes go for walks around the skete. Fr. Isidore was watched in every possible way in order to prevent him from entering into a conversation with the Metropolitan. Although they kept an eye on him, it seems that once they weren't watching close enough. Abba met the Metropolitan and said, "I have something to tell you, Batiushka. They say in the newspapers that there is hunger in India; the Indians are starving and yet we have lots of everything. Send some money there from the Lavra's funds." Wishing to avoid any further contacts like this between Fr. Isidore and the Metropolitan, the Metropolitan's cell attendant took some precautions: "If'n Fadder Iz'dore comes 'round, don'cha let 'im in."

Not long before his death, the Elder once again came into conflict with everyone. Here's how things went: an argument arose between the Vyksa Iveron Icon Convent—founded by Elder Barnabas—and the skete where Fr. Barnabas lived, as to where the body of the founder should be buried. Barnabas himself had requested that he be buried in the convent he had built, but the skete wanted to preserve the Elder's body within its walls. Then priests from the Iveron Convent went to the royal court, where it was asked which of the brothers were for the removal of the body from the skete and which were against the idea. Only two old men voted for the removal of the body—one of whom was Fr. Isidore.

And even when he was dying, Fr. Isidore remained true to himself. Just before dying, and without worrying about his own illness, Fr. Isidore came to one of the older brothers, who was entrusted with caring for the brothers' needs, and who—as was said—was noted for his hard-heartedness. The Elder gave him an icon of the Mother of God called "The Softening of Hard Hearts." In this one gift, everything was united: tenderness for one's brother, the desire to act on hard-heartedness with kindness and to turn to the prayerful intercession of the Mother of God, as well as a firm yet gentle hint to the brother about his sins.

As always, gentle Fr. Isidore was not afraid of confronting something, yet his confrontations were done with such love that the one being confronted could hardly ever imagine getting angry at him.

CHAPTER 9

in which the writer attempts to relate Fr. Isidore's asceticism to the reader.

If you, O reader who are tolerant enough to read this story, should wish to know something about the great Elder's *podvig*,[18] then to the best of my ability I will try to recount all that I know. But you shall see that Fr. Isidore concealed all of his podvigs under a blanket of great silence—as if in the inner desert of his innermost self. In the old days, a certain brother, having arrived at the skete to see Abba Arsenius the Egyptian and having peeked in through the doorway, saw Elder Arsenius as if aflame and was terrified by the vision. Likewise, we can contemplate Fr. Isidore's deeds only secretly taking a look through the gate to his "Inner Desert." Anything that I'll be able to say will be only incidental and quite fragmented.

Fr. Isidore never interrupted his state of fasting, and constantly fasted by abstaining from words. He would always abstain from food and drink, of course—for want of food and drink. Indeed, he himself never had anything, and if something was brought to him, he would give it away to someone else: not only that which was brought, but even his very own meal at times. He partook of the little he did have, however—not to take pleasure in the natural and rightful sweetness of the food, but on the contrary, to exchange its good taste for a

18. *Podvig*: spiritual struggle or ascetic endeavor.

worse one. As he himself would say, "It's impossible to ruin that which is already completely good." You have already learned about the preserves which Fr. Isidore would cook for himself, as well as his salad. But in this chapter listen to a tale of Fr. Ephraim, *Hieromonk*[19] of St. Sabbas of Zvenygorod Monastery, about raspberry preserves.

"I was not in the least bit surprised," wrote this spiritual son and friend of the late Elder, "that no matter how often one would ask the fathers of the skete about Fr. Isidore's life, each one found it difficult to say something clear which would offer the possibility of learning something about this Elder as an ascetic. Outwardly, it is hard to discern the actual asceticism found in the following occurrence.

"During my stay at the St. Sergius Lavra, I remember, once during the Dormition Fast,[20] Fr. Isidore arrived at the Lavra from the Skete of the Paraclete. He came by to see me. I prepared some tea and began offering him things to eat. Along with the tea, I served some raspberry preserves of superior quality. The Elder had some preserves with his tea and remarked, 'These preserves are indeed very good. They say that they are good for the common cold.' I responded, 'Yes, raspberries are known as a means of warming one and making one sweat.' I then invited him to take the whole jar back with him to the monastery. With a slightly inquisitive look on this face, Father glanced both at me and the jar and said, 'That's quite a large jar (it contained 5-6 pounds of preserves). It would be a pity not to take a few to store up for the winter.' I carefully wrapped the jar up in some newspaper, then tied the paper up with a napkin, and Father carried it home in a bundle, along with various other supplies.

"The very day following the Elder's visit, we had beautiful, real summer-like weather. Hieromonk Theodore, a priest from the Lavra who is also sincerely devoted to Fr. Isidore,

19. *Hieromonk*: priest-monk.
20. August 1st to 15th.

and myself had made up our minds to take a drive to the Skete of the Paraclete to visit the Elder. We arrived and, as usual, knocked on the door of the cell, while offering a prayer. The door then opened and Father greeted us with his angelic and light-filled, good-natured smile: 'Dear guests! Welcome! Welcome! How quickly we missed each other! Why don't we walk on over to the wooden tree stumps? I can bring the samovar along and we can have some tea.'

"Suddenly, just by chance, on a shelf under the canopy I saw the jar of preserves which had been given to the Elder just the day before—less than half full, and with slices of fresh cucumber mixed in with the preserves that remained! Not being able to restrain myself, I cried, 'Batiushka, this is a sin! Shame on you for ruining such fine preserves by shredding cucumbers in them!'

"The Elder good-naturedly responded, 'And what about you—getting all worked up and irritated! It's impossible to ruin that which is already completely good . . . the only thing you can really do is just enjoy it. . . . And thus, I've divided it up into two parts.'

"I then asked, 'Where did you divide up the preserves? Into other jars?'

" 'Yes. Here is how I divided everything up: yesterday as I arrived back home from visiting with you, I put some preserves in a teacup and took them to our elderly blind monk, Fr. Ammon, and I also gave a little bit to Ignatius the canonarch, as well as a bit to Johnny the bell-ringer—all friends of yours, aren't they?'

"I then answered that I had never heard of those people.

" 'Well, I told them that Sergius (Fr. Ephraim's legal name was Sergius) had given them these preserves, and that they should remember him in their prayers. . . . Then everything would be fine.'

"I then replied, 'But Father, didn't you say you wanted to save the preserves for winter?'

" 'And you keep saying the same thing over and over. . . .

Go on over to the tree stump to have some tea. I'm sorry that there's nothing else left to offer you as a little treat: we weren't expecting you to drop by today.' "

That's the kind of fast the Elder practiced. But he valued prayer even more. He lived, breathed and was fed by prayer. He continually repeated the Jesus Prayer, as Elder Abraham testified.

In a corner of his "Inner Desert," he would often pray for hours, kneeling in worship on a big stone, in imitation of St. Seraphim, the Miracle-worker of Sarov. He would be at each Vespers service and each Liturgy, kneeling in worship on the cold floor, in the lower level of the temple of St. Philaret the Almsgiver. He continually remembered our Lord Jesus Christ and often, with deep contrition of heart, repeated the Prayer of His five wounds, which the reader will become acquainted with later on; that is, if the writer receives God's blessing to complete this story.

However, one does not even know what to say about the most important aspect of Fr. Isidore (by this I mean his podvig of prayer). Breathing is necessary for man, but if you were asked to talk about the breathing of your father in the flesh, would you have a lot to talk about, dear reader? Not much, for breathing is quite natural to man. In just this very way was prayer quite natural to Fr. Isidore. We wouldn't notice this inhalation of God's grace going on inside of him, in exactly the same way that you wouldn't notice the inhalation of air by your father in the flesh. Another thing is that your father in the flesh breathes air, but our father in the spirit breathes grace: once or twice a day, or moreover per week. Yet that is not how the Elder's life of prayer really was. It was apparent to everyone that Fr. Isidore never ceased praying, whether he was in a conversation or dealing with household chores; however, no one ever dared to ask him about this. Yes, to tell you the truth, these inquiries seemed useless and unnecessary.

CHAPTER 10

the purpose of which is to point out Elder Isidore's abundant spiritual freedom to the reader, and also to tell how the Elder broke a fast.

Fr. Isidore's deep humility did not allow him to be insensitive to other people's opinions. Indeed, his spiritual freedom in no way denied the reality of his asceticism. Truly, Father recognized that *the Son of Man is also Lord of the Sabbath* (Luke 6:5) and that *the Sabbath was made for man, and not man for the Sabbath* (Mark 2:27). He was no longer under the letter of the law, but was free. He lived according to rules; yet when it came to church rules and regulations he knew the difference between the letter and the spirit of the law. If need be, he would freely and resolutely break the letter for the sake of preserving the spirit. This is why one could hear the following opinion of Fr. Isidore expressed: "I never saw anything special in his life. . . . He didn't live an especially strict life: he made use of everything. He used to go to the bathhouse, though moderately. He wouldn't shun the bathhouse and used to go there. He didn't disdain a little wine, either."

But occasionally, even direct violations of the rules took place.

Thus, once on a fast day, Elder Abraham went to visit a certain family. The family made an offer: "Wouldn't you like some fried eggs?"

"I'm afraid not," refused Fr. Abraham.

"But we just gave Fr. Isidore some fried eggs to eat."

So as not to cause any unpleasant feelings in his hosts, Fr. Isidore had broken the fast on a fast day.

The Elder would repeatedly say, "It's better not to stick to one's fast, if by denying food one would insult another."

Another time, both Elders were together in the same home. Once again, it was a fast day. The Elders were offered some butter. Fr. Isidore spread some on some bread and ate it, while the other Elder didn't accept that which was offered.

"Aren't you going to have anything to eat?" asked Fr. Isidore.

"It's Friday, you know!"

"I insist that you have something to eat."

"I'm not your spiritual son!" objected Elder Abraham.

Once during the first week of Lent, the Elder himself informed the Bishop, "Batiushka, absolve me from my sin. I broke the fast during the first week of Lent."

"How's that?" questioned the Bishop.

"There was a little milk left over and it was a shame to waste it, so I drank it."

So Fr. Isidore broke his fast twice during the first week of Lent and this happened just a few years before his death, when he was already well advanced in years. But who knows how these events are to be understood? Perhaps he was disciplining himself for the final humility? Or—as is quite possible—perhaps he was teaching humility to his fellow man?

Fr. Isidore never refused wine. He would say, "To insult someone with a refusal is much worse." When offered, he would drink a glass of wine with his meal and sometimes have another half glass; in his old age he would have three, but would never consent to drink any more, for whatever reason.

The usual prayer rule, it seems, was not followed by the Elder. The Bishop once asked him, "Which rule do you follow, Father?"

"I don't have any rules at all," answered the Elder.

"How come you don't? You yourself used to serve with ecclesiarchs [who enforce the rules] ."

"That's how come I don't. When I was on Mount Athos (Fr. Isidore once lived on Old Mount Athos) and asked an Elder about the *typicon*,[21] he said, 'What typicon do you mean? I myself don't have one at all. Here's a rule for you: repeat constantly, "Lord, have mercy." If I were to give you a long prayer, you'd forget it, but you won't forget this one since there are only three words.' Such a simple rule," concluded Fr. Isidore, smiling, "but I can't even fulfill *that.*"

However, one has to understand the meaning of these words. Fr. Isidore did not at all reject the typicon, for he himself recited not only "Lord, have mercy," but many other prayers as well. His answer expressed his great humility and freedom of spirit, with which he taught others.

Sometimes he would leave the skete without asking permission. One of the Elders related: "A hermit, Fr. Alexander, was staying with us. Fr. Isidore was very close to Fr. Alexander—they confessed their sins to one another. Fr. Isidore had a more gentle way of dealing with sin. Here's what would happen: you would meet him outside the skete and ask, 'Batiushka, have you requested permission to leave the skete?'

" 'You be quiet.'

"Once Fr. Isidore and I asked permission to go visit Bishop Evdokim, but the Abbot did not allow us, saying, 'He will laugh at you; I will tell him.'

"But afterwards Fr. Isidore said, 'The Abbot has his own politics.' And he continued visiting the Bishop."

So, dear reader, you can see just how free in the spirit Fr. Isidore really was, even when during a confession, with his epitrachelion on his neck and a cuff on his arm, Father would leave to check on the samovar, while the penitent remained alone reading a list of sins which was pasted on some cardboard.

---

21. *Typicon:* rule of church services.

Remaining above the world, Father could always enter the world without incurring any harm. He didn't despise the world, didn't disdain the world, nor did he have any fear of it; he simply carried at all times the strength within himself which allowed him to remain above the world, and to accept it into his consciousness as something pure. The temptations of the world had no allure for him; and its fascinations did not tempt his pure heart.

A certain Fr. Ephraim (whom we have mentioned before) once recalled that he entered his cell and spotted a novel by Paul de Kok on his table. Fr. Ephraim guessed that one of the monks had placed this book there as a joke. But at that moment, Fr. Isidore arrived and admitted, to Fr. Ephraim's great surprise, that he himself had placed the book on Fr. Ephraim's table.

"Are you aware just what kind of book this is? Where did you get it?" the dumbfounded Fr. Ephraim asked Fr. Isidore. Fr. Isidore then explained that one of the brothers had brought it to him, probably as a joke.

"And since you are a very learned man," Batiushka said, turning to Fr. Ephraim, "I decided to hand it over to you."

"Well, it's rather indecent."

"Oh, don't worry about that. Go on and read it. Toss out whatever is bad, and retain whatever is good in your heart," retorted the Elder.

That's what a free spirit Fr. Isidore was. He had a gentle approach towards everything, without any tension, almost as if playing. And in each spontaneous movement of the spirit you could feel his power—larger than all the forced attempts and efforts made by others.

That's how he was with everyone. But what he did would always remain between him and God, and only his Heavenly Father could comprehend it.

CHAPTER 11

which informs the reader what occurred during confession with Fr. Isidore.

No matter what time of day one came to Fr. Isidore, he would never refuse to hear one's confession. Moreover, if he were asked, he would never refuse—despite being weighed down by his age and illness—to go to someone's home to hear a confession, or to Posad, even though the distance between the skete and Posad was well over two miles.

One Elder recalled: "People with all kinds of sins would constantly swarm around Fr. Isidore. They were outlaws . . . all types came—even those with their swords. It was a dangerous time for him during the uprisings.[22] Revolutionaries would come by and say, 'Look, we have slain so many people with our swords; it was not our own doing, we were only following orders.' Fr. Isidore kept his courage; he could promise forgiveness from God for everything. I watched as some of these men left carrying their swords—I was familiar with these people."

—"Batiushka, you spoke of how someone had slain people with a sword?"

"He was a soldier."

Even up to a few days before his death, hardly having the strength to sit up in bed, Fr. Isidore continued hearing confessions.

22. That is, during the revolutionary movements. (*Author's note*)

The desire of the penitent to cleanse himself—that is what Fr. Isidore turned his spiritual glance to during confessions; he gave few admonitions of any kind. The Elder's spiritual simplicity softened even the oldest wounds of the soul. He himself once recounted, "All kinds of people come to me. A man carries a sin around with him for twenty years—but to me he reveals it."

Even at the simplest encounter with Fr. Isidore, his glance would somehow warm the disordered soul and bring it calm, as if piercing it with a gentle ray of sunshine. Whenever someone's soul was impure, Fr. Isidore would meet the sinful brother and look him straight in the eye—and it was impossible to look him straight in the eye for very long due to his radiant glance. That's why a certain man with a troubled conscience fell on his knees before Abba and requested a prayer, though he was seeing Abba for the first time. One of the skete monks spoke of his encounter with Father in the garden: "He took me by the hand and looked me straight in the eye. . . . It seemed to me as if he could see through everything. I raised my head and then lowered it again, and he said, 'Peace be with you, Mikey.' "

Usually Fr. Isidore would hand people making a confession a special list of sins which he would have them read aloud and ask them to make a mental note of those sins which they had committed. Sometimes Fr. Isidore—in his tattered old epitrachelion and his dilapidated only cuff—would even leave the lay brother in the middle of a confession and go to prepare some refreshments for his "sinner."

He would never get angry: if there was sin, he would grieve with you but would not get angry at you. He dealt with everyone calmly, simply and fairly, and would lovingly say, "You should pray more." He would especially recommend that one turn to the Mother of God for protection. But he would invariably point out to each one the reality of the Prayer of the five wounds of the Savior and would teach how it should be prayed.

The Elder's confession, although outwardly simple, was as special as an elusive breath of eternity. Usually during confession you see a man before you. But in his case just the opposite was true: the person confessing would find himself not in the presence of a man, nor even a witness for the Lord, but in the presence of Eternity Itself. There was not the slightest sign of complaint or reproach, nor a single movement on the Elder's face. There was no special inquiry, either. In short, each person making a confession firmly knew that he had landed in the Kingdom of Freedom.

That was the attitude towards all laymen, and in general to all those outside of the skete brotherhood.

In the skete, however, Fr. Isidore was not the official Father Confessor for all, although earlier, in the course of eight years, he used to confess the hieromonks. But it would often happen that the Spiritual Father appointed from the skete, in the hope of correcting one or another brother, would treat a brother rather roughly, and would even throw him out, saying, "Do not come to me anymore."

The guilty brother would be ready to lapse into despair or to become embittered and then, with a sorrow-filled soul, would run to Fr. Isidore for help. Father would accept everyone, and one glance of his would soften any despairing or embittered soul. But the official Father Confessor of the skete got angry at the Elder who had acted in defiance of his intentions, and he even complained to the Abbot, saying that in such a way it was impossible to correct brothers. But Fr. Isidore, not paying any attention to this prohibition, could not help but receive all those who came to him to repent; and, seeing the despair, he acted from love and not with severity. He would not weigh these people down with heavy penances, but on the contrary would try to comfort them, cheer them up, calm them, and bring peace to their souls. One of the brothers was a bit fond of the bottle at times. Fr. Isidore took him and drove out the evil despair and hopelessness from within him.

But a different situation also occurred. It would happen that people came to Batiushka, not simply because they had been driven away by the Father Confessor, but just because they wished to avoid the expected penance. The Elder accepted these people too, but would always fix some kind of penance. "This," he would say, "is for the double sin: for running away from the Confessor, and for that which the brother came to repent of originally."

Once one of the brothers had eaten bologna: someone had offered it to him in the Lavra, and he could not resist it. The brother then became afraid to go to the Father Confessor and instead went to Fr. Isidore and told him what had happened.

"What did you do, eat it all?" asked Fr. Isidore.

"Eat it all? I only ate three tiny slices."

"O.K. then—300 prostrations."

"Why, Father? . . . Just because of the three tiny slices?"

"No, otherwise I won't forgive you. Go to the Confessor then. 300 prostrations."

"I only ate a bit. They offered me. . . ."

"That's for the double sin: for the bologna and for wanting to avoid the Confessor."

But in this strictness of the Elder there was much gentleness: Fr. Isidore knew that the Confessor would appoint more than 300 prostrations. So the penitent had to accept the appointed penance.

CHAPTER 12

which contains the "Talk of the Rock," i.e., the narration of a certain professor's visit to Fr. Isidore and what came of it.

Once, dear reader, a certain professor called upon the writer of the story you are now reading, and he began to tell of a visit he had made to Fr. Isidore and how the Elder had heard his confession. The memory of this confession strongly disturbed the professor's soul; for a long time he couldn't seem to find the appropriate words, and he would repeatedly return to the beginning of his story. After a while, he succeeded in stopping his tears, which had continually welled up at the thought of Fr. Isidore, and was able to somewhat collect his thoughts. Then—still not satisfied with his own words—he requested his listener to write the narration set out below, which he called:

"Talk of the Rock"[23]

who?

23. This monologue is valuable as an illustration of the Russian intelligentsia's "return to Orthodoxy" during Elder Isidore's lifetime. Many of the intelligentsia, looking down their noses at the "popular piety" of the masses and at "backwards" monks and clergy, could only accept an abstract and idealistic Orthodoxy of their own devising, one that would suit their high opinion of themselves. The aristocratic professor who narrates "The Talk of the Rock," however, is forced to reevaluate these prejudices of the intelligentsia when he comes face to face with Elder Isidore. His comical, pedantic posing is contrasted with the humility and clearsightedness of the unlearned Elder.

"I fear sounding like the intelligentsia," he began. "I fear that my words may only give the impression that Fr. Isidore simply appealed to an intellectual. This is not so. . . . The essence of the matter is that I (part professor, part intellectual, part sick, write whatever you want . . .) ran headlong into this Elder, and nothing seemed to be between me and him, between me and Christ. I went to the Elder, satanically hardened with church problems, fed up with politics, Bishops, Merezhkovsky,[24] the Theological Academy and all its professors. But no matter how many rationalizations and how much malice I brought with me, it all melted away in Fr. Isidore's cell. But after that the same thing occurred: I became sick again. Yet to the smallest detail, down to the vivid image of his clothes, his eyes, and so forth, the memory of this 'shock' remained and still remains something solid. The cell, the flowers—there was no scent in the air. The air was pure. I breathed freedom. I am not able to describe the cell—I usually don't remember details—yet there was something terribly bright, pure and light in the cell—something totally remarkable.

"Now I have somewhat gathered my thoughts together and will recount my visit in its natural sequence.

"I entered the cell, already knowing what a cell was like. I was fifty years old. I had seen monks and priests, and knew them well. I arrived with a feeling of formal humility, having been sent by the Bishop to his Confessor. The point is not that I was just comforted by the first priestly ignoramus I ran into—and I emphatically recognize a priest as my father and

24. Dmitri Merezhkovsky was a popular figure of the Russian "Silver Age." A founder of the infamous Russian Religious-Philosophical Society of Petersburg, he gained a following among the liberal intelligentsia by probing spiritual, metaphysical and ecclesiastical questions. His search for something "new" caused him to deviate far from the Orthodox Faith, for which he was criticized by Florensky. Like Tolstoy (to whom Florensky compared him), Merezhkovsky wrote highly original novels, using them as a forum for his false ideas.

judge in matters of confession and interpersonal relationships. No—the point of the matter is this: I entered into the little cell, located in the corner of the monastery, together with a friend. I was struck by the clarity, the purity, and the simplicity of all that surrounded me. I had assumed that everything would be as it had always been in the past—that a courteous, decorous monk would courteously receive me and that I would courteously confess to him, and then everything would be as prescribed. But that's not what occurred: it suddenly seemed to me that this cell, in all its simplicity, was infinite power. I myself didn't know of what that power consisted, and with all my doubts I began telling myself: 'You're dramatizing, you're nervous, you're imagining pictures. . . .'

"At that point the old man, clearly remembering (as I know now) who I am and what I am, greeted me like a stupid and uncouth monk. In our talk—which lasted several minutes—, whenever I wanted to prove or explain something, I saw that I could not explain or relate anything to him. And then I saw that if I, having just entered his cell, would begin explaining to him, he would humbly and clearly reply that I was more knowledgeable than him in theology, philosophy and in everything—and that I knew things far better than he did, all the way from philosophy to catechism. And what power brought me to him, the Elder, as if to seek and inquire after something? Then I felt that I had come to seek something else entirely, and I simply began to cry. To my weeping, the Elder answered with a prayer that 'those who weep shall be comforted.' Once again I understood that this reply— and prayer about 'those who weep'—had to do with me: 'Here is what I shall give you as an answer—what you could have answered yourself, since you came to me in want of a catechetical or homiletic response.'

"Once again I became ashamed. That's when I was definitely convinced that the grace of God had brought me right where I needed to be. I then asked the Elder to hear my confession, as well as that of my friend who had come with me. It was right then that I experienced what I call my impression of the Church.

"The Elder rose and—just as he was dressed, with his shirt outside his trousers—he stood there quietly and said, 'Well, fine.'

"He took out his epitrachelion and placed it on himself; then he energetically affixed an old velvet cuff onto his shirt sleeve and said, "Blessed is our God." Then, turning to me and my friend, he asked that we begin by reading Psalm 50, the Creed, and prayers. I could barely read this Psalm and prayers, although I knew them in three languages—stumbling from word to word and feeling that, when I was corrected, a power was supporting and guiding me.

"When we had finished reading the prayers, he gave me a little book in which I could read the standard confession of sins. During this, he looked at me and my friend standing next to me and told me with his glance that he didn't need my idle talk and details, and that I should just read—together with the brother standing next to me—whatever was written here, while repenting and recognizing that which I hear and see.

"I was ashamed that I was involuntarily emphasizing the individual words of the confessional prayer. It seemed as if the Elder was telling me: "Why is all this emphasis necessary? Why do I need a clever person like you, with all your logic and understanding?'

"When he finished reading the prayer of absolution, I could only say one thing to him: 'I have something on my soul now —I myself don't understand why. . . .'

" 'Christ is risen from the dead.' Then he continued singing: '. . . trampling down death by death, and on those in the tombs bestowing life.'

"I then began crying again, and he told me again that I would be comforted; and when I left, he kissed my hand.

"I know only this: that I saw the Rock upon which the Church was built, and that all my problems before that moment were dismissed.

"Besides the greatness of this moment, there's not a whole lot more I can say. It has always remained with me as an incredible shock. The Church opened itself up for an instant and later closed its doors again: the Church—in baggy pants, a golden cuff and epitrachelion—upon a Rock. There has never been anything like it. Perhaps Fr. Isidore was indeed an 'insignificant' Confessor—as is the accepted opinion—and not popular. I have known and seen Confessors and Elders—all of whom were *muzhiks*[25] and 'know-it-alls,' as they say. But as far as this case is concerned, I, an aristocrat, saw none of these traits in Fr. Isidore. None of my attempts at definition were sufficient concerning this matter. And again I repeat: 'He is neither this nor that; he's more than all of this put together.' He was not a Barnabas (I didn't know him myself, but heard that he allegedly knew how to get muzhiks to make sense in their confessions). He was not the refined Confessor, the likes of whom I had seen all too many times in Moscow. He was average—that is, something truly great that can't be reduced to any definition.

"I know one Bishop. He too is full of grace. But you have to force him, you have to force the grace right out of him. Yet with Fr. Isidore, there was something unusually light. So as to clear up any misunderstandings, I will once again clarify my words:

"He was unusually light and simple, like the so-called muzhik-priests. I know perfectly well how easy it is to make a confession with whatever country peasant, fool, or 'Black Hundred' member[26] you like. But after confessing to them, you are left feeling still self-satisfied, feeling that there is something about you they cannot understand and that you have no right to demand this understanding of them.

"But such was not the case here. Here—lightness was

---

25. *Muzhiks*: Russian peasants.

26. "Black Hundred": a derogatory term for anti-revolutionary groups in Russia, active 1905-1907.

straightforward and direct. This absence of a double curtain is a terribly rare thing.

"All my impressions are summed up right here: I, an intelligent and educated, learned man, am familiar with all the conventions with which one can approach another soul wishing to make a confession. And I have certainly witnessed all of these conventions: yet none of these were to be found in the soul of Fr. Isidore."

With this the narrator ends his story.

Chapter 13

in which the reader learns what Elder Isidore taught in his talks with others.

Abba Isidore did not like to make admonitions and he did not like to reason like a scholar. And not only was he himself careful to not do so, but he stopped others from doing this too. "Don't be too curious about this type of thing," he would say. "It's dangerous for a monk to be too curious." He spoke sternly, however, of the *Dogmatic Theology* of the Metropolitan Macarius of Moscow, and had this to say about its writer: "He himself sank in all of it," i.e., the attempt to squeeze living faith out of the hand-vise of reason.

That's how cautious Father was with regard to faith.

"I was somewhat embarrassed at their prejudices," (i.e., those of Fr. Isidore and Fr. Barnabas), recounted a certain Elder.

—What prejudices?

"Those typical of common folk. Fr. Isidore and Fr. Barnabas—they don't know anything. They don't comply with Macarius' catechism. And I have heard Fr. Barnabas reprimanding Metropolitan Macarius. They don't know how to separate dogma from morality. Dogmatic Theology is one thing and Morality is another; but there is also Comparative (Accusatory) Theology."

The Elder who had spoken these words was right in his own way. Actually, Father was never schooled in theology; he had a spiritual life in God and received his spiritual authority from God. In living with God, it was impossible to draw a boundary line distinguishing the various subjects of schooling. Each sequence of things which caused division into books, chapters, departments and subdivisions disturbed Fr. Isidore's soul, because a different order reigned in his soul—an order that was understood not through teachers and professors, but by the Holy Spirit. And one often would have liked to ask about Abba Isidore: "How does he know the Scriptures if he has never studied them in an Academy?"

I repeat to you, dear reader, that Abba Isidore's strength didn't lie in wise words, but in the spiritual strength which accompanied his words, even the most ordinary ones. If you're still curious as to what Fr. Isidore would talk about, then I will provide you with several examples; however, when reading them you should firmly keep in mind that Fr. Isidore's words are to be seen as independent of the one who speaks them, since they contain almost nothing "Isidorian" in them, and fade like the little flaxen flower when torn from its stem.

"I remember," recalls Fr. Ephraim (whom we have already mentioned), "I remember when some letters from Metropolitan Philaret to the Archimandrite at the Lavra, Anthony, came out from the press (in a book entitled *The Resolutions of Metropolitan Philaret),* and in one of them I read a note addressed to the Archimandrite: 'Isidore answered well.' At the first opportunity I had, I turned up at Fr. Isidore's and asked him what on earth he had answered the Metropolitan; and the Elder told me the following:

'Three of us appeared at the Metropolitan's for ordination: I, who was to be ordained to the priesthood, and two other monks, who were to be ordained deacons. The Metropolitan began talking with the younger ones and, turning to the very youngest, he asked, "By what do you hope to be saved?"

' "Humility," the youngest monk answered.

' "And do you have a lot of that?" the Metropolitan said. And he went on to ask the other, "And by what do you hope to be saved."

' "Your holy prayers," was the answer.

'The Metropolitan then got angry. "Where did you learn to be so hypocritical?" he said. And then he asked me, "And by what do you hope to be saved?"

'I answered, "By the suffering on the Cross and the death of our Lord and Savior Jesus Christ."

'The Metropolitan crossed himself and said, "Memorize this answer and remember it always." ' "

That same person (Fr. Ephraim) wrote the following about Fr. Isidore: "He was imbued with a deep understanding of the dogmatic truths of the Holy Orthodox Faith, and to questions concerning the same he would always give completely correct answers, based upon the writings of the Holy Scriptures and the Holy Fathers of the Church."

Fr. Isidore spoke mostly of the Mother of God, the Church, and of the suffering on the Cross and the death of the Savior. This, by the way, did not pose any divisive questions for him, but somehow combined very well together.

He would often compare the "birth" of Eve—the mother of the human race who was taken from Adam's side—to the "birth" of the Mother Church, taken from the side of Christ. Fr. Isidore equated Adam's miraculous sleep to the mysterious sleep of death of our Lord; the ribs taken from Adam were compared to the piercing of our Lord's side with a spear; the miraculous flowing of blood and water from the wounds of Christ he saw as being timed to coincide with the very birth of the Church. And somehow this birth of the Church coincided, in his way of thinking, with the wound in the heart of the Mother of God from the piercing of the weapon. For Fr. Isidore, the suffering of the Mother of God was somehow connected with the grace of the Church. "Christ gave birth to the Church," he would sometimes interject, "and we became united together."

The peak of Fr. Isidore's theology was his Prayer to Jesus, in which a hint of these thoughts could be found. The reader will become acquainted with this prayer in the next chapter.

The Elder honored and loved God's Saints, and his feelings toward them were deep, heartfelt and alive. The Elder's heart was always with the Saints—he was close to them, as close as to his own dear ones, and even more. But Fr. Isidore had particular esteem for Saint Seraphim, the Miracle-worker of Sarov, for Monk George the Recluse, for Tikhon of Zadonsk, and still others. He quite regularly referred to these carriers of God's grace in his talks with others: the Elder didn't like to talk on his own behalf.

Often, with deep affection, he would repeat the words of Saint Seraphim: "O my joy, my joy! Acquire the spirit of peace and thousands of souls will be saved around you."

If any conversation was filled with idle or angry words, he pointed to the power of the word and often recalled the verses of George the Recluse:

> The word is the spark of the soul in me.
> Now rush, my soul, to eternity.

In departing he would often say:

> With soul shall I convince my soul:
> If kept from idle words and wrath,
> I'll find the theologian's path.

And sometimes he would say the verses in another way, such as:

> With soul shall I convince your soul:
> If kept from idle words and wrath,
> You'll find the theologian's path.

Fr. Isidore loved to use a lot of animation while reading a collection of verses from one of the Psalms, which he had read in some magazine and which had highly pleased him. On these occasions he would light all up, and would read with much expression and force. Sometimes he would even place a thick little book in the hands of his guests—a collection of Psalms in verse, compiled by some blind priest. Having turned his attention to the latter (he was blind, you know!), he would

ask someone to read his rather contrived verses out loud.
Derzhavin's ode called "God" was recalled several times.[27]
But most often, and with great warmth, he would speak of
N. V. Gogol and by heart he would say the verses compiled
by Gogol in a prayer to the Holy Virgin. He would first
pronounce the epigraph quickly: "No one who comes to
Thee will ever depart from Thee still feeling deprived, Most
Pure Virgin Mother of God, but will ask for grace and will
receive this gift upon a worthy petition."

Then he would begin this prayer itself:

O Holy Mother, pure and blessed,
To Thee I dare my voice to raise, etc.[28]

For some reason he particularly loved this prayer. Likewise,
he recalled the prayer verses on the Cross of Christ:

With wondrous strength is the Cross invested.
Its splendor nothing can excel, etc.

One of his favorite prayers was the following one in the
works of Holy Hierarch [Hieromonk] Dmitri of Rostov:

H	Hear, my Jesus, Sweetness to my heart;
I	In grief is joy—the twain are not apart!
E	Exclaim to me: "The end of sins am I,
R	Redemption's rock and door that leads on high!"
O	O God, Thy virtue comes and clings to me;
M	Mercy, love—for these we raise our plea.
O	Oppressed, I know not whom my soul can find,—
N	None will come save Thee, my Lord most kind.
K	Kept in Thee, my needs are held akin;
D	Do also let me keep Thee deep within!
I	In me abide, make manifest Thy grace.
M	Much have I sinned—I long for Thy embrace!

27. See "The Orthodox Word," Vol. 18, no. 4 (111).

28. This and other prayers are to be found further on in the Appen-
dix. (*Author's note*)

I	In pain, without Thy love, my life will fade:
T	Thou art my strength, in Thee I'm not afraid.
R	Rejoicing with the great Angelic Host,
Y	Yearning for their realm, in Thee I boast.

But most often Fr. Isidore would invite his guests to join with him in singing the "Blessed art Thou" verses from the Burial Rite of the Mother of God, which rite was performed in the Gethsemane Skete on the 17th of August, for the Dormition and the Ascension of the Holy Virgin Mother:

"Blessed art Thou, O Sovereign Lady; enlighten me with the light of Thy Son.

"The assembly of angels was amazed, beholding Thee, O Most Pure One, among the dead: Thou Who didst give Thy soul into the hand of God, Thou Who in Godly glory didst depart with God into heaven," etc.

That is how the gray-haired Elder Isidore sang to the Virgin Mary. And upon finishing the verses, he would ask his guests to write them down for themselves and to sing them more often at home. Fr. Isidore constantly repeated that purity, peace and gentleness were from the Mother of God, and that She, Who had suffered so much Herself, would come to help those who called upon Her.

He would never fail to ask his guests if they had been to the underground church of Our Lady of Chernigov, and if the guests replied that they hadn't, then Father would ask that they go there to pray.

Whenever two friends came by to see Fr. Isidore, he would always express his joy and approval at seeing their friendship, but at the same time he would persistently repeat each time that it was necessary to live in peace.

"Brother will strengthen brother, and thus the city is well guarded," he would conclude, precisely foreseeing the possibility of a rupture and a falling away from one another.

Whenever someone would complain to Abba about some sickness and misfortune, the Elder—almost with envy (if you will permit me to use this most unsuitable word)—would say, "You see how God loves you—how he remembers you."

One brother was sick. Elder Isidore met up with him and asked, "Well, Mikey, how are you getting along?"

"I'm not well, Batiushka."

"Don't you know that if God comes to you in the form of some sickness or misfortune, this means that He loves you? The Lord is calling on us with sicknesses, and this will be a substitute for virtue."

The author N. V. Gogol (†1852), to whom
Fr. Isidore attributed his much-loved poem
to the Mother of God (see pp. 143-4).

Opposite page: Schema-Abbot Herman (†1923).

Above: Hieromonk Barnabas (†1906).

Together with Fr. Isidore, these two formed what
Florensky called a "threesome of holy Elders."

Archimandrite Anthony (†1877),
who came from the same village as Fr. Isidore,
and for whom Fr. Isidore once served as a
cell-attendant.

CHAPTER 14

the most instructive chapter, since it teaches the reader Fr. Isidore's grace-giving Prayer to Jesus, which gives not a small amount of spiritual comfort to each person who begins to read it with understanding.

No matter who came to visit Fr. Isidore, Father would teach each one to recite a Prayer to Jesus which he had composed, or rather, which was revealed to him from on high.

Father himself would continually use it. The Elder attributed much importance to this prayer (which the attentive reader will read a bit further on) in the struggle with one's own thoughts, and he believed it to be filled with abundant power. One might suspect that he himself had learned it during a vision. Father, however, would not elaborate on the origin of the prayer, although with much insistence he would advise everyone to recite it.

This Prayer of the five wounds of the Savior and the weapon in the soul of His Virgin Mother most of all helps in meeting such needs as the consolation of the soul, the curbing of one's short temper, malice and anger, and the chasing away of lustful thoughts and passionate dreaming. That is what the Elder would say, and as proof he would sometimes refer to how this prayer once shook off the evil spirits which had prevailed over a woman.

The Elder would recite this prayer, turning his face towards the icon triptych. He would pronounce the first part very slowly, as if with a certain kind of expectation, while looking at the holy Crucifix. During the reading of the second part he would contemplate the icon of the Virgin Mother while reading rapidly, with animation and joyful expectation. Once he would say this short prayer, the Elder's outer appearance would be transformed. It was as if some kind of light would shine forth from his eyes, and all of him would light up with a festive kind of joy, the kind which you can only come to know from "The Song of Songs" or from "The Marriage of the Lamb of God" in the Revelation of St. John the Theologian. The grace-giving effect of the prayer was first of all evident in the person himself.

He knew this. That's why he would so very often ask others to receive a treatment with this remedy.

"Cross yourself consciously—like this—and temptation will pass," he told his visitor when the visitor complained to him about temptations, sadness or affliction. At this time the Elder crossed himself, and recited the Jesus Prayer. "If you ever have a need, then say this (then follows the prayer), and turn to the Mother of God. She is purity itself; She loves purity—and will help you."

With such and similar words, Elder Isidore convinced others to pray the Prayer of the five wounds of our Lord Jesus Christ and the weapon in the heart of His most pure Mother the Virgin Mary. But while the Elder was alive, for one reason or another, this prayer was poorly learned by both skete brothers and laymen alike. This was something surprising: it wouldn't seem to stick in anyone's mind, even though it was quite simple and short. Certain brothers rather improperly read as if they were some kind of uneducated "simpletons" when they recited the prayer. Therefore, the Elder taught the prayer to every educated person he would meet.

"He composed the prayer himself," said one of the brothers. "He would drop by so-and-so's place; I was amazed at his boldness. Wherever we were visiting together, he would always seem to bring out his prayer and notebooks (i.e., the leaflets which were already mentioned earlier)."

That is how it was while the spirit-bearing Elder was still alive. But just when he left this world, many who suddenly remembered that they didn't know the Prayer of the five wounds, began writing it down for their own use in prayer, and others learned it by heart. Many were witness to the great and abundant force of Fr. Isidore's prayer, especially with regard to impure thoughts and idle daydreaming. "The Prayer of the five wounds of our Savior is so powerful," said one of the brothers of the hermitage—from his own personal experience, "that demons haven't the slightest chance against it."

So here for you, gracious reader, is this last earthly gift from our aged Elder, Fr. Isidore. Read it then for the health of the body and soul, and teach it to those dear to you, for the sake of the memory of the Elder, through whose prayers the Lord will have mercy upon you.

PRAYER OF THE FIVE WOUNDS
OF THE SAVIOR[29]

which Elder Isidore taught his spiritual children to pray

Where does it hurt?

Placing the hand on the shoulder, say:

LORD, Thou Who art crowned with thorns upon Thy head, to blood and marrow, for the sake of my sins;

---

29. The initial words from each line of this prayer comprise the first phrase of the ancient Jesus Prayer: "Lord Jesus Christ, Son of God, have mercy on me, a sinner." The last sentence is based on the words of St. Simeon the God-Receiver to the Mother of God when She brought the Christ-child into the temple (Luke 2:35).

Lowering the hand to the right foot, say:

JESUS, whose right foot was pierced with an iron nail for the sake of my sins;

Placing the hand on the left foot, say:

CHRIST, Whose left foot was pierced with an iron nail for the sake of my sins;

Raising the hand to the right shoulder, say:

SON, Whose right hand was pierced with an iron nail for the sake of my sins:

Transferring the hand to the left shoulder, say:

OF GOD, Whose left hand was pierced for the sake of my sins; and Whose side was punctured by a spear; from Whose side flowed blood and water for the redemption and salvation of our souls;
Through the Mother of God, grant me understanding.

Turning one's face towards the icon of the Mother of God, say:

—And through Thee Thyself, through Thy soul the weapon pierced, so that from many hearts will be revealed a spring of the repentant, thankful and heartfelt tears of all mankind.

CHAPTER 15

written with the aim of letting the wise and humble reader know of Elder Isidore's gift of clairvoyance and his performing of miracles.

Is there any need to remind you, gracious reader, that neither the gift of clairvoyance nor the gift of performing miracles or any other such gifts do not—in themselves—instill the Spirit of God in man? Being a good Christian, you will of course constantly ponder the fact that the Kingdom of God is righteousness and peace and joy in the Holy Spirit, and not miracles or prophecies or healings—which many God-wise ones spoke of in the writings of the Fathers of the Church. You are already aware that one who loves God and seeks the Kingdom of God will receive, along with the Holy Spirit, His gifts as well. And the Savior said: *Seek ye first the Kingdom of God, and all these things will be added unto you* (Luke 12:31).

In truth, that's how Fr. Isidore was. He never sought after those things which would make most people marvel, but rather, like a certain very wise merchant, would first of all recover the precious pearl of his soul (Matt. 13:45). God reigned in his soul, and with God came the spiritual joy and abundant life promised by the Savior to His disciples. But this living water, which poured out abundantly from Isidore's transparent heart as if from a crystal vessel overflowing at its brim, created signs and gave the Elder this invisible power.

For those who had visited the Elder, there was no doubt that he saw and knew the innermost secrets hidden from man. All the same, these obvious gifts didn't have any effect on Abba himself, for who would start looking at the furniture of a king's palace in the presence of the king himself? And Father didn't readily talk about his own spiritual gifts, because he considered them a natural result of life in God. Therefore, whenever he was asked about his clairvoyance, he would calmly answer, "God is with us. He is near to us and He sees with our eyes."

Not once, not twice, nor even three times, but time and again, many of Abba's disciples were convinced that whenever they visited Abba, he would be the first one to begin talking about the matter for which they had come to see him. You would arrive and he would greet you with an opinion about the very same thing that you had wanted to ask him about. Such occasions seemed so common for the Elder's disciples, that no one ever bothered writing them down and now they have disappeared from memory. But here, for example, are a few such stories which by chance have survived for the edification of those who never got to see the Elder:

Someone had gone far away from Sergiev Posad, and on his return home a most unexpected meeting took place which disturbed him very much. What happened was this: the man saw the wife of one of his friends and she told him of her husband's grave moral condition and despair. The man could have gotten off the train at the next closest station and gone to see his friend, but for one reason or another such a thought never entered into his head—or perhaps, as they say, it was hidden by the devil's tail. Once having arrived at Sergiev Posad right in time for the Liturgy, this same man suddenly understood, during the divine service, that he had to go back quickly in order to make up for his omission. And just as the train was leaving for that city deep in the night, this same person found time to get off to go to Elder Isidore's for a blessing.

The weather was starting to act up when he approached Father's little house. Father met him at the door and, even before being able to give a blessing, he said to the man who had not approached him yet, pointing to the snowflakes whirling about in the air, "Look! Look! Good things do indeed fly around, just like flies! You have to go quickly—otherwise the trains might be stopped by the snow." Then Father confirmed the necessity of leaving that same night; he blessed and even wrote a letter to the one in need in his shaky, old man's clumsy handwriting.

Here is another story: a certain spiritual son of Fr. Isidore (by the name of Fr. G.) once came by to see the Elder in order to make a confession, after which he gave the Elder two rubles. Fr. Isidore took the money. Then a sudden thought flashed in the mind of the one who had given the money: "Why on earth would he take that money, knowing how poor I am?" Fr. Isidore did not respond in any way to this thought. But during a further discussion, a poor man came by whom Fr. Isidore had already asked to come back in the evening for some money, even though at that time there had been no money at all. Father gave the two rubles to this petitioner and added the following: "You see, a good man came by to give you this money." Then, accompanying Fr. G. to the door, he said to him privately, "Don't regret that I took two rubles from you: prayers coming through them—through lay people—reach God far more easily than from you or me." Fr. G. interpreted this happening as an unquestionable case of clairvoyance.

If one came to Fr. Isidore with sin on one's soul, if one had had a disagreement with someone close, or a cooling-off of love, then Batiushka himself would always begin talking about this; or, after he would ask two or three questions, one would be forced to confess and repent. This became such a common occurrence for everyone that whenever someone persisted in sinning, he tried not to let his eyes fall on the Elder.

Life in the other world was a common life for the Elder. He

would quite often have dreams of the Mother of God, Saint Seraphim and other Saints, and he heeded their divine inspiration. Here, for example, is how Elder Isidore's acquaintance with Bishop Evdokim began:

"Before 1904 I had never met Fr. Isidore," recounted Bishop Evdokim, "although I had heard a lot about him while still a student at the Academy. Our first meeting took place in May of 1904. It was a marvellous day, and I had gone out into the garden of the Academy. Shuffling towards me was a bent-over old man, with a walking stick, and wearing a skull-cap. He greeted me and said, 'Batiushka, are you the Bishop?'

" 'I am. And what can I do for you?'

" 'I am Fr. Isidore.'

" 'Pleased to meet you.'

" 'I'm here on business: last night the Mother of God appeared to me and said, "You still haven't asked for a blessing from the new Bishop?" So here I am. . . .' "

Due to his elevated state of mind, Father also understood the signs of all of God's silent creation. He would repeatedly tell, for example, how in his hometown there had appeared in church a ball of fire which had burned the iconostasis, and in this ball of fire Father had seen the wonder of God; and because of this he had left the world.[30] And lightly smiling, the Elder would unfailingly add, "Well, perhaps they'll say that it happened all by itself. But I think differently. . . ."

And that's how it was in fact. Other free thinkers (by whom our beloved reader should not be tempted) would say in a scientific way that this was most certainly a "ball of lightning." But what does that mean? Cannot God speak to us through balls of lightning? In His hands rests all of creation, which He uses to speak to us; but our hearts have grown hard and we do not understand God's language. Batiushka Isidore, however, heeded all of creation; for him the word of God sounded in all creation and therefore the whole world for the Elder was filled

30. I.e., had become a monastic.

with marvellous signs and mysterious inspirations. For this spirit-bearing man, the ball of lightning was a miracle; the earthly soul would not even see the end of the world as a sign from God. The profane, who have desired to live without God, are punished by having the eyes of their hearts grow dim; they neither see nor know God and do not understand the signs of His anger, and therefore nothing will push them to take a look at themselves and repent; they live as in a dream, yet even this dream they cannot understand, and they take their fantasies for displays of truth.

That's not how the Elder lived at all. He was always sober and cheerful in spirit. He listened to God's creation and God's creation listened to him. Invisible threads united him with the hidden heart of creation. Not only was the world a sign for Elder Isidore, but the Elder himself was a sign for the world. And truly, things happened to the Elder which never happened to other people.

He himself spoke, for example, of one such instance: on the day of the Dormition of the Mother of God—when women are not forbidden entrance to the skete—a certain woman once came to him and complained about a constant headache. "You must make the sign of the Cross with understanding," said the Elder to his visitor, and he taught her his Prayer of the five wounds of the Savior. The woman had just begun to make the sign of the cross and had just barely raised her hand to her forehead, when she began trembling and fell to the ground in convulsions, with black foam coming out of her mouth. Batiushka managed to bring this woman from the skete to the underground church of the Mother of God of Chernigov. There the woman received a healing from her illness.

CHAPTER 16

concerning the cross that Fr. Isidore bore and how little those around him really understood him.

The whole of Fr. Isidore's life was not an easy cross to bear, yet the Elder patiently carried his cross. From this bearing of his own cross, perhaps more than anything else, Fr. Isidore possessed his own special, other-worldly type of peace, from which he derived his force and strength. A life in God seems possible to us only when certain conditions are·realized; we maintain our equilibrium when we enjoy public esteem, when we are prosperous and enjoy other such similar and perishable riches, which to St. Isaac the Syrian, our father among the Saints, were equated with pus. But for Fr. Isidore, faith was a living, self-acting force which never forsook him. With him, everything was just the opposite of what it is with us.

As a former house-serf in a manor, he never spoke one bad or bitter word concerning his former master. Even less: while the princess was still alive, he would visit her annually, bringing prosphora and a string of bagels.

He would tell about how he was persecuted by having to work very hard—yet with such matter-of-factness and with such a joyful smile, as if the matter was not about him. And he was persecuted always and everywhere. He was forced to leave Old Mount Athos because he did not have any money. In the Skete of the Paraclete, he gathered the children of some neighboring peasants together, offered them tea, taught them prayers and gave them a few kopecks from his poor man's means.

This did not please the authorities at all, and rumors began spreading that Fr. Isidore drank heavily and brought women to his place. Finally, after some fabricated story had been pegged on him, he was chased from the Skete of the Paraclete and moved back to the Gethsemane Skete.

He was constantly subjected to persecution in his life. And why was this? Because he confessed brothers who were ready to fall into despair due to the severity of the Father Confessor; because he took in strangers; because he gave bread to the poor; because without asking permission he went to the village outside the city walls to comfort someone; and because he was too forthright with the authorities.

The more the young brothers loved him, the more disdainfully the older brothers would deal with him—with very few exceptions. They did not care at all for his independence and straightforwardness and found them to be unbearable, in spite of the Elder's great humility. The absence of ostentatious fasting drew scorn to him as to a vagabond and drunkard. But it was the Elder's simplicity that did him the most damage in the eyes of the brothers, who had the opinion that they were educated and considered his simplicity to be "ignorance." Some of them considered the Elder strange, a kind of fool and somewhat deranged. They would call him an "odd ball"—and that is when they would express themselves rather mildly.

Fr. Isidore was a monk for sixty years and during that time he never once received a priestly award. The eighty year-old Elder lived alone in his hut and had to do everything with his own hands, for there was not one assigned cell attendant. He was so neglected that while he was ill his face was covered with layers of dirt; and Bishop Evdokim, who came to visit him, found lice in his gray hair. It was only six days prior to his death that the Elder received some help.

Poverty, ill health, scorn, insults, persecution—the Elder's path in life was strewn with such thorns. Yet even with those thorns he maintained such an air of peace, such joy, such a full life, the likes of which we ourselves do not possess and do not acquire under the most favorable conditions.

What was the most remarkable thing about Batiushka? Without a doubt it was that in each situation he remained a Christian. His Christianity was his very element. It wasn't worldly nor was it tied to his actual social condition. For him, Christianity was not just the bloom of life, but was life's very essence; it was not an embellishment on life, but was life's very nucleus. Misunderstood during his lifetime, the Elder, it seems, has remained misunderstood even after his death. Up till now, those who knew him still have not contemplated just what a treasure they have lost. But the Elder's resplendent light continues to shine in the night of miscomprehension.

CHAPTER 17

in which some scant information concerning Elder Isidore's life is brought to mind; his place of birth, the remaining years of his life, and the spiritual influences which the Elder experienced.

And now, dear reader, you know what kind of man Abba Isidore was, and therefore you probably wish to learn more about how he came to be the way he was. To satisfy your curiosity, I will inform you of a few things about the Elder's life which I know.

Abba Isidore was born in the village of Lyskov in the St. Macarius district of Nizhegorod province. In Holy Baptism he was named John. His parents were peasant servants in the house of the Prince Gruzinsky: their names were Andrew and Paraskeva, and their surname was Kozin. Subsequently, John would always give his surname in two ways: sometimes Gruzinsky and sometimes Kozin—but usually Gruzinsky. John's exact date of birth is not known. According to information from Elder Abraham at the skete, John was born in the same year that St. Seraphim, the Miracle-worker of Sarov, passed away. John himself, not long before his own death, repeatedly spoke of an unforgettable talk he had with his mother on the day of St. Seraphim's death. "A wonderful frangrance was given off," he said. "I asked Mother where it came from, and Mother told me: Elder Seraphim had passed away." In two or three days news came of Seraphim's death. If we base ourselves on the first account, then John's date of birth would have to be 1833. But if we accept the second account, then we have to conclude that by 1833 John was already a considerable number of years old, for only then could he have remembered the events of that year; then, as John himself believed, his date of birth would be set in 1814.

In any event, a ray from St. Seraphim's radiance entered into John's life. Even when John was still in his mother's womb, his mother went to Sarov to see Elder Seraphim. The holy man called her forth out of the vast crowd of people, bowed down before her to the very ground, in front of all the people present, and prophesied that from her would come a great ascetic, and that his name would be Isidore. And subsequently, at the skete, Fr. Isidore maintained exceptionally close ties with one of Elder Seraphim's disciples.

Very little is known about John's childhood, adolescence and youth—only that which he himself spoke of. Of primary importance here was the significance that the Gruzinsky Princes' home theater had in his life. He played "Filka" and a few other funny characters; it seems that love for poetry and art was awakened in John at this same time. But despite his taste for such worldly pastimes, the young boy never forgot his soul. Even then he was yearning for a monastic podvig.

"Father and Mother would be busy with household chores in the evening," the Elder recounted not long before his death, "and I would turn towards the wall and look at the picture of Saints Zosima and Sabbatius (of Solovki Monastery) and would see green meadows and monasteries."

One sign turned these youthful thoughts into a firm decision. Once, young John was praying in his hometown, in the Church of the Feast of the Protection. Lightning appeared during the full moon—as the Elder himself later described it—and, shining brightly, it shot past the iconostasis and burst into thunder. Nothing happened to any of the people there; only the iconostasis turned all black. This sign (the old-timers still remember it) had an effect upon John. As one of the brothers expressed it: "Lightning struck—and it warmed him up."

"I thought about going to Athos," said the Elder. However, this thought was not successfully realized at that time, and John entered the Gethsemane Skete which had been established by Metropolitan Philaret. There, once again, he met his fellow villager, Archimandrite Anthony, who also came from the village of Lyskov and was a stepson of Prince Gruzinsky.

At the same time one should remember that, judging by certain facts (in particular, the surname "Gruzinsky" which John carried and called himself, his slender build, and finally his somewhat Eastern nose and face), one could suspect that John had more noble roots. It was not at all improbable that he was of royal stock.

Archimandrite Anthony accepted John as his cell attendant. At that time John was still a young boy with no beard or moustache. He assisted the Archimandrite, and in a semi-uncial style he wrote a list for the commemoration of the living and the dead. He also read in church and sang with a gentle bass in the choir. It was here that he met Fr. Abraham, who afterwards served as cell attendant in his place under Fr. Anthony. It was at the Archimandrite's that he saw Metropolitan Philaret of Moscow several times, as well as many other remarkable figures of that time.

At first, Archimandrite Anthony was very friendly towards Br. John; perhaps family ties contributed to this friendship. But afterwards their friendship grew cold. The Archimandrite grew closer to Metropolitan Philaret and committed his intellect to ambitious projects. But Br. John told the Archimandrite much truth and, most importantly, he reminded him of the past—of the time when Anthony was a medical assistant at Prince Gruzinsky's. The Archimandrite became heavily burdened with this fellow villager and said, "He became a bit too much for me."

The period that Fr. Isidore considered the real beginning of his podvig was a particularly special time in the history of the skete. There were those still alive who could recall the Miracle-worker of Sarov. A whole throng of true monks shone their light into the world from the depth of the woods where the skete now stands; many important people from the laity came to enlighten their souls and to gain strength and courage. At that time there was no brick wall around the skete; they lived apart and each one there carried out his own special struggles. A group of the ascetics went to live underground and they dug out an entire cloister with a church and even a well. At the ringing of the underground bell, these monks—with candles in hand—would leave their sepulchre-like dark cells, which were so tiny that they were barely able to lie down completely outstretched in them, and would gather in narrow, damp underground passageways for evening prayers. They would read Psalms and sing alleluias and then disperse to their own cells. It was very stuffy in the underground church, and thus wooden tubes were extended outwards from the church in order to bring in some fresh air. Sometimes in the evening you could hear the monks and Fr. Anthony singing through these tubes. At times, Metropolitan Philaret also lived in the skete.

In 1860, Br. John was tonsured and took his monastic vows at the same time as Fr. Herman, now called the Schema-Abbot of Zosima Hermitage, which is located just behind the Skete of the Paraclete. The Elder of the hermitage, Fr. Alexander, accepted both of them—i.e., John (his monastic name being Isidore) and Herman—as his spiritual sons, which Barnabas (who died in 1906) had also become not long before.

Worthy of attention is the coincidence that this threesome of holy Elders—Isidore, Herman and Barnabas—turned out to be so spiritually tied to each other. It was during this time that Fr. Isidore, as Elder Alexander's firstborn spiritual son, was looked up to by them as being the eldest; and therefore at Fr. Alexander's death he assumed the position of spiritual father to his orphaned younger brothers.

At this time, the Skete of the Paraclete did not yet exist.

When it was erected—for those who wished to live a life of strict seclusion—Fr. Isidore moved there, too. It was here that he quickly became a hieromonk. In 1863, he was ordained a hierodeacon, and in 1865 a hieromonk. He never went any higher than this; the schema,[31] which they offered him due to his age, he refused out of his humility.

This was at the same time that Fr. Isidore planned to go to America with Bishop John to preach. It seems that the Archimandrite [Anthony] had sewn a new fur coat for him for the long journey; but for one reason or another the trip never took place, and the fur coat took off for America without its owner. Nearly five years after entering the Skete of the Paraclete, Fr. Isidore realized his longest-held wish—to go to Old Mount Athos. He spent one year at this historical breeding ground of monasticism. During that year, the Athonite Elders one day came up with the idea to erect a cross on the very top of glorious Mount Athos. Fr. Isidore actively contributed to the erecting of our Lord's Cross.

However, for lack of enough money to acquire a cell for himself, Fr. Isidore had to leave the monastic republic within a short time and return to his homeland. He once again settled in at the Skete of the Paraclete—but this did not last long, for he underwent persecution, slander and expulsion. He then moved back to Gethsemane Skete where he lived without interruption until his very blessed end.

Out of all the events of this time, it's worth mentioning Fr. Isidore's appointment as spiritual Confessor to all the priests, when he took over following Fr. Barnabas' death in 1906.

31. Schema: strictest monastic rule in the Orthodox Church.

CHAPTER 18

which informs us of Abba Isidore's blessed repose.

That is how Abba Isidore's quiet life passed by. And his end was incomparably quiet. One could even imagine that he just didn't die, but simply fell asleep gradually. His breathing grew more and more faint and finally ceased completely: he breathed one final breath and with this breath his life flew away.

Even up to the very last minute of his life, he maintained his usual joyfulness and clear awareness, remaining an abstainer even on his deathbed. Even his ability to recall faces, names, quotations from spiritual verses, and the various personal circumstances of different people, never lessened. His illness—hemorrhoids, diarrhea and hemorrhaging—was excruciating, yet he never complained to anyone about it. Whenever he was asked about his health, he would answer—with his invariable smile: "It's all right, glory be to God. It's all right. Everything is fine." His body was emaciated, and his hands were like two dried twigs covered with skin. His sickness wreaked great havoc upon his body. His face, which was usually so full, was dried up and thin; his cheeks were sunken, which made his nose more pointed. At the end, the Elder didn't even have enough strength to smile. Only his eyes—Batiushka's clear, bright eyes—still shone like bright stars, with an amazingly radiant light. While Father's weakened body still lay in this world, his eyes seemed to shine already outside it. Whoever had the honor of seeing them knew just what a blissful end really was.

The Elder's sickness had already begun a while before; yet it became even more noticeable around Passion Week in 1907. By the feast of the Dormition in 1907 his hemorrhaging increased so much that the Elder was forced to stop attending divine services, except for partaking of Holy Communion.

From Advent on, he was completely bedridden and it was already possible to foresee the fatal outcome of his illness. Abba would eat next to nothing, and therefore grew even weaker. For the last seven days of his life he would only sip a little cold water from a teaspoon.

During the final days before his death he fervently and persistently taught those who came by to see him, repeating his favorite thoughts. Most of all he would repeat his Prayer of the five wounds of the Savior—which is already known to the reader. Continually reminding everyone of the poor, he would say, "Those who have should give to those who have not." He would also say, "A righteous man will instruct a sinner through mercy," and, "A kind man will lend freely to God, and God will pay for everything." He would ask his superiors to be sympathetic to the poor and the sick—to church people as well as to the lay people. Concerning mercy, he said, "Mercy is praised at the Judgement."

He continued showing interest in church affairs and repeatedly talked about unification with the Old Catholics, saying that no one should pride himself on who is to be first; and he pointed out once again that the presiding chair at the council would be filled by the Mother of God. He bade his farewells to the brotherhood and to his spiritual children. He gave a commission to each one, saying that those who were under his care should help one another; he asked that they not forget the poor; he distributed his meager possessions and gave a blessing. To one he gave the commission to convert a ruble into small change and to give it to the needy.

It was evident that this farewell to the world fatigued him greatly, with his body already half dead, as it were—yet he didn't want to stop these final activities. When just three days before his death he was paid a visit by his spiritual son Bishop Evdokim, who asked him if he feared dying, Father answered, smiling, "No, I'm not afraid. Whatever for? Glory to God—it's all right. Glory to God—it's all right." He gave minute instructions, taking care so as not to let the smallest possessions of his poverty slip his attention. He then told the Bishop to take whatever he pleased: he gave him his staff and shorter mantle. Although not even able to move, he suggested to him: "Come, I'll confess you." Disregarding any excuses, he then heard the confession and, with the words, "I am going away," he gave the Bishop his confessional book, which was torn and greasy from long use. Even on his deathbed the Elder recalled that it was necessary to render a service to his spiritual son. He remembered and said to the cell attendant, "I have six potatoes over there. Divide them up among the poor." He gave similar instructions concerning some remaining jam and even took the trouble to allot a slice of bread.

To Fr. Israel the Elder said, "I had wanted them to lay me to rest in my epitrachelion. And then I felt guilty: it's way too good. You can ask the monk in the vestry for another epitrachelion—a poorer one—to put on me, and take this one to His Eminence (i.e., Bishop Evdokim)."

And the epitrachelion which Fr. Isidore denied himself was ancient, worn out, soiled and falling apart. For his whole life Fr. Isidore confessed with it; for his whole life he would not part with it. Yet before death, even with this he parted. This was the highest sacrifice of love, for we cannot even imagine what this epitrachelion meant to the Elder.

On February 2nd, two days before his death, at 4 o'clock in the morning, Fr. Isidore wanted to partake of Holy Communion. After an early Liturgy, at about 6 a.m., they came to him with the Holy Gifts and gave him Communion.

A cell attendant then said to him, "Batiushka, you're really dying!"

"Enough, enough," Fr. Isidore expressed tenderly. "Have you thought about what you are saying? With God there are no dead—everyone is alive. 'He that believeth in Me shall never die.' . . . I'm not dying. . . . 'God is not a God of the dead, but of the living.' "

On the following day at 2 o'clock, two students from the Theological Academy dropped by to see him, bringing ten rubles with them. Fr. Isidore ordered a cell attendant, Br. John, to give him a small box in which he placed the money and instructed that it be divided among the poor. After a while, still lying down, he asked the cell attendant, "Brother, go and ask the Confessor to come."

The Confessor arrived at 7 o'clock in the evening, took a look at the sick man and said, "You're pretty bad off, our dear, much-needed Batiushka."

Father answered, "I don't feel good; that's why I want to receive Communion. If I make it through the night, come on my name-day." (the 4th of February was his name-day and he remembered this).

The Confessor left at about 8 p.m.. Br. John, who was still by Father's side, began reading the *Lives of the Holy Fathers* and the Gospel to Fr. Isidore. Having glanced at Father, Br. John noticed that he was fiddling with his fingers and said, "I'll clip your fingernails!" But Fr. Isidore replied, "Tomorrow."

When the cell attendant began once again to read the Gospel, Father said to him, "Br. John, hand me the cross."

After the cell attendant handed him the cross, Fr. Isidore crossed himself with it, gave a blessing to Br. John and then handed it back.

Once again, Br. John read from the Gospel for awhile, but then noticed that Fr. Isidore had taken a turn for the worse. The cell attendant requested forgiveness and prayers from the Elder, and then began reading the Gospel again. But

Fr. Isidore interrupted him, saying, "Br. John, put out the light."

But the cell attendant did not fulfill this request and asked simply, "What for, Batiushka?"

Fr. Isidore began breathing rapidly and said once more, "Put out the light."

Then Br. John blew out one icon-lamp and went out into the hallway, because Fr. Isidore had said to him earlier, "Don't watch my end: when the great Anthony lay dying, he sent his disciple for some water while he himself died. While Saint Seraphim lay dying, the door to his cell was locked and then he died. So it is with all God's servants: no one has seen their end. And you, too—go read a book or go to bed."

While he was still healthy, Fr. Isidore had told his disciples that it is even a sin to look at how a man is dying; he had referred to St. Paul of Thebes and many other saints. The Elder's demand that the light be put out was not a sudden whim. No, it was a long-held, ripe and mature conviction that when you die, you have to be completely concentrated, entirely free from all worldly things, and you must prepare yourself inside and remain at one with God.

What precisely the dying man was doing in these last minutes, what precisely he was feeling and thinking in his silence and inner peace, which was not disturbed by the usual sight of the lowly cell and the humble flickering of the icon-lamp—not only is it impossible for us to find this out, but even if we could, it still wouldn't be in our power to comprehend it with our minds. Abba's soul could do that which is inaccessible to our understanding. But, brother reader, what is remarkable is that—in his great humility—at the moment of his death, face to face with God, Fr. Isidore compared himself to those spirit-filled ascetics and used such expressions, as if this comparison was the most natural of things. In someone else this would be imposture and intolerable impudence. But coming out of Fr. Isidore's mouth, a little boldness seemed so natural that it passed by almost unnoticed. This pre-death tes-timony, given by Batiushka regarding himself, has great value for us; for who could evaluate this spirit-bearing man and understand him any better than the Elder himself?

Thus, Br. John put out the light and went away. Batiushka was breathing heavily. Br. John lay down on the floor in the hallway, fully clothed, and began to doze off while listening to the breathing of the dying man. It was 9:30 p.m. Having snapped out of his drowsy state, he suddenly leapt up on his feet and listened. It was quiet inside the cell. He approached Father. The Elder's mouth was wide open. Br. John felt the body; it was still warm. Then he understood that the Elder's soul had departed to God. It was 11 o'clock in the evening. Br. John ran to wake up Fr. Israel. The latter arrived and performed the last rites.

Therefore, at 11 o'clock in the evening of the 3rd of Feb-ruary, 1908, on the eve of his name-day, the great Elder of Gethsemane Skete passed away. He was, most probably, about 84 years old.

CHAPTER 20

which informs the truth-loving reader of the honorable burial of Elder Isidore, what his face looked like after his blissful and tranquil departure from life in this world, as well as a description of his gravesite.

The next day, news of Fr. Isidore's passing spread throughout the Sergiev Posad and even reached Moscow. On February 5th, at around 8:00 a.m., the Elder's vast spiritual family gathered in the skete church of Philaret the Almsgiver for a final farewell. Bishop Evdokim was also present, as were members of the Moscow hierarchy, the monastic brotherhood, several students from the Theological Academy and other laymen; even some women somehow found their way into the church, although they weren't allowed access to the skete. It was a triumphant occasion, yet very sad too, for it was painfully felt by everyone that such a firm support, the likes of which we'll never see again in our lives, had gone away. Here and there people wept bitter tears. The Bishop officiated at the service.

When they finished singing the service, the Bishop beckoned to those people who were closest to the deceased to come up to the coffin. A tight ring of people surrounded the Elder's coffin. The Bishop then gently lifted the black cloth from Batiushka's face.

The Elder was lying there as if he were still alive—although his face had grown thin—without the slightest sign of decay. It was as if the hand of death had not touched him.

A light smile lit up his closed mouth; it still seemed as if his chest was breathing. A deep peace and stillness emanated from this coffin—not just a feeling of a cold grave, but a cool, fresh fragrance of a bright evening. In his coffin, the Elder was like a setting sun over whitened, ripe cornfields. It was not the majestic silence of a dead man, nor the solemn absence of the reposed, that could be seen there, but rather a blessed peace in God: Fr. Isidore was here, sleeping, not at all fear-evoking, not at all terrifying —but was very, very quiet and very, very meek. When he was alive, one glance of his would always bring comfort and peace. But never had Fr. Isidore been like this before. With the *klobuk*[32] pulled down over his ears and his head tilted a little to the left, appearing clear and bright (and not deadly pale or waxen), he was lying there looking indescribably handsome. You would feel like asking him for a blessing and tears would fall from your eyes of their own accord—no longer from anguish or grief, but from a single, pure feeling of tenderness, contrition and exultation before the beauty that has conquered death. This was the first coffin we had ever seen from which there was no eeriness. And in it lay "a flesh-bearing spiritual beauty"—if the reader will allow me to recall the words of St. Gregory of Nyssa—, the beauty of the Sabbath of Christ's entombment.

When the funeral services had ended and all those in attendance had bade farewell to the Elder, Bishop Evdokim gave a eulogy over the unpainted pine coffin: this treasure which the Gethsemane Skete had been fortunate enough to get. He spoke briefly about Elder Isidore—things which the reader is already well aware of—and he then began to define the late Elder's place in relation to the history of monasticism. The Bishop pointed out that this Elder was the last flower of the ancient Thebaid, the last representative of monasticism. "We don't have real monasticism at present," the Bishop approximately said, "It still has to be created. Fr. Isidore

---

32. *Klobuk*: headgear of the Orthodox monk.

was a forerunner of the monasticism which is yet to come, and which began in the far off Thebaid. Amen."[33]

Oil was then poured on Fr. Isidore's body. The coffin was quickly nailed shut. Overwhelming weeping resounded from many elderly people who were co-ascetics of the deceased. Batiushka was carried to his final resting place, along the road leading past his little wooden hut, at which a *Litya*[34] was served. It was cold and snowy. After a short while the sky began to rage and the wind picked up once again. But, despite the cold wind, no one wanted to leave this yellow hillside located near the chapel in the brotherhood's cemetery. The winter passed. Spring came and went, too—a spring without Fr. Isidore. Towards the summer, his gravesite was cleaned and covered with grass. Some flowers were planted and a wooden white cross with black lettering was placed over the grave, along with a ruby-colored icon-lamp with an eternal flame.

This is how the cross looked on top of that priceless grave: On the face side of the cross was written: "Under this cross lies the body of the slave of God, Hieromonk Father Isidore. Tonsured in the skete in 1852. Died in 1908, on February 4th. His age was. . . ." (The number was deliberately erased, for it had been written incorrectly).

Inexpensive icons were hung there: icons of St. Seraphim, St. Theodore, the Mother of God of Chenstokhova, a copper crucifix, and others—all of which were voluntary offerings from unknown admirers of the blessed Elder.

---

33. Bishop Evdokim's statement, although containing a vital truth that Florensky elucidates in the next chapter, also contains an obvious exaggeration and betrays the Bishop's tendency to want to "renovate" Orthodoxy. This tendency resulted, after the Russian Revolution, in the Bishop's abdication of monasticism and traditional Orthodoxy altogether. For further commentary on Bishop Evdokim's statement, see the Introduction, p. 34.

34. *Litya*: a brief memorial service for the dead.

On the back side of the cross was written: "Lord, receive my spirit in peace."

On the cross there hung a glass lantern made from tin and painted green. In it an icon-lamp burns, just as unquenchably as burned—like a lamp before our Lord Jesus Christ—Elder Isidore.

CHAPTER 21

this is the last chapter, and if the reader is in want of time, he may skip it as it doesn't contain any new information on Elder Isidore.

Once a certain brother asked St. Niphon of Constantia: "There has been an increase in the number of holy men throughout the world today. Will it be so in the last days?" To such an inquiry, the blessed one answered: "My son, Prophets of the Lord God will not be in scarce supply in the last days, yet the same applies for those who serve Satan. However, in the last days those who truly work for God will successfully separate themselves from the world and will not perform signs and wonders for people as at the present time, but will walk the path of life opened up by humility, and in the Kingdom of Heaven will find themselves greater than the fathers who were renowned for their miraculous works; because at that time no one will perform miracles before the eyes of men which could spark people and awaken them to the zeal of striving to do ascetic labors. Those who serve at the altars of the priesthood all around the world will be completely inept and will not know the art of virtue. The same goes for monks to come; for all will be brought down by gluttony and vanity and will serve more as a temptation than an example for people. Therefore, virtue will be scorned even more; greed for money will reign, as well as sorrow for those monks who have become rich with gold, for they will become a disgrace to the Lord God and will not see the face of the Living

God. . . . Therefore, my son, as I have said before, many—being afflicted with ignorance—will fall into the abyss, becoming lost in the great expanse of the wide and broad path."

Such was the prophecy given by the Hierarch of Constantia. And behold, remembering Fr. Isidore, you will be compelled to repeat to yourself the prophecy of old: "In the last times the holy ones will succeed in hiding themselves from the people." This prophecy has an even greater impact upon the soul when you meditate on the words of Fr. Isidore, that the last days are approaching and are indeed very near and that there will soon be such persecution that Christians will once again be forced to go underground.[35]

Indeed, Fr. Isidore in his spiritually wise simplicity knew how to conceal himself not only from the world, but even from those in the brotherhood closest to him, as well as from the monks with whom he lived. There was nothing really remarkable about Father, or rather Isidore, but what indeed was remarkable was that there was nothing remarkable.

He was in truth one who bore the Holy Spirit. That is why the remarkable thing about Fr. Isidore was—and continues to be—his elusiveness to our descriptions and his intangibility to our intellect. Whole and complete in himself, Abba would appear to be an absolute contradiction whenever we would try to express him in words or to say, "There . . . he's like this or that." Yes—he practiced fasting, but at the same time he broke his fasts, too. Yes—he was humble, but at the same time he was independent. He had renounced the world, yet at the same time he loved all of creation, like no one else could. Yes—he lived in God, yet he still read newspapers and occupied himself by reading little poems. He was meek, yet could be severe at the same time. In short, to one's intellect he was a continuous contradiction. But to the pure in mind, he was as

35. It will be remembered that the author wrote these prophetic words in 1908, a decade before the bloody Russian Revolution and the Soviet attempt to liquidate Christianity.

complete a person as you ever will find. Spiritual wholeness often appears as a contradiction to the intellect. He was in the world, but not of it. He never neglected anyone and always remained in a heavenly state. He was spiritual, was filled with the Holy Spirit, and through him it was possible to see just what Christian spirituality and a Christian "other-worldliness" were all about. It wasn't for nothing that the respectable and experienced Elder of the Gethsemane Skete, Fr. Barnabas, had Fr. Isidore as his spiritual father and even called him "a second Seraphim"; and Elder Abraham, who had labored in the "caves" and who had already been living at the skete for 55 years, said that Fr. Isidore "generally displayed a dove-like meekness." "I have never met anyone like this Elder," confessed many of the brothers.

Much more could still be said about Fr. Isidore Gruzinsky, but a longer narration would probably only serve to exhaust your patience, patient and gentle reader. Forgive me then, the unworthy compiler of this story, if due to my poor lack of skill the Elder's fragrant appearance does not come across in these writings. Having extolled our Lord God for the miracle he gave to us in the form of Elder Isidore, I now lay down my pen in extending my brotherly gratitude to you, as to some true fellow traveller of this common path we walk, along a spiritual meadow, in pure, healthy air bursting with fragrances. May a quiet peace descend upon your soul, dear reader—a peace similar to that which unceasingly and abundantly shone in Elder Isidore, and may the unfading light of joy continue to shine within you. Amen.

The End
of the Narrative about Fr. Isidore

APPENDICES

Leaflets which Fr. Isidore handed out.

I.

A prayer, composed by Gogol, to the Blessed Virgin. Fr. Isidore loved to recite this prayer. It is not to be found in the Complete Collection of the Works of N. V. Gogol, *yet according to Fr. Isidore it was printed in* Russian Archive, *1899, Book 8, by A. A. Tretyakov, and in the* Moscow Gazette, *1909, No. 65. Fr. Isidore himself learned it from his own brother, who was a valet in the home of Counts A., P. and A. G. Tolstoy (Moscow, Nikitsky Blvd., presently the home of the Katkovs), where Gogol lived the last years of his life and died.*

"No one who comes to Thee will ever depart from Thee still feeling deprived, Most Pure Virgin Mother of God, but will ask for grace and will receive this gift upon a worthy petition."

O Holy Mother, pure and blessed,
To Thee I dare my voice to raise.
My face with tears is washed, caressed:
Attend the words my heart conveys,
Accept this passionate petition,
Save me from misfortune, wrath,
Fill my heart with sweet contrition
And set me on salvation's path.

May I be free, with Thy direction,
And be prepared to give up all.
Through bitter times, be my protection—
My death from utter grief forestall.
Thou refuge for all those in need,
Our intercessor with the Lord!—
O, shelter me when all pay heed
And judgement strikes all like a sword,
When agelessness breaks into time,
The final trumpet wakes the dead,
And burdens of my every crime
From books of conscience shall be read.
Truth's wall Thou art, its vindication!
With all my soul I pray to Thee:
Save me, O my consolation,
And with Thy love encompass me!

II.

The verses, "Blessed art Thou," in the 5th tone, are sung in the Geth-semane Skete on the 15th of August—on the Dormition of the Most Holy Mother of God. Fr. Isidore often repeated these verses and encouraged his disciples to sing them, both alone and together.

"Blessed art Thou, O Sovereign Lady; enlighten me with the light of Thy Son."

The assembly of angels was amazed, beholding Thee, O Most Pure One, among the dead: Thou Who didst give Thy soul into the hand of God, Thou Who in Godly glory didst depart with God into heaven.

"Blessed art Thou, O Sovereign Lady; enlighten me with the light of Thy Son."

"Why, O you preachers of God, do you mingle joy with tears?" The Twin, enlightened from above, arrived and unto the apostles did cry: "Behold the sash! and understand that the Virgin has risen from the grave!"

"Blessed art Thou, O Sovereign Lady; enlighten me with the light of Thy Son."

The disciple, O Sovereign Lady, who believed not in the resurrection of Thy Son, now does assure others of Thy rising, saying: "The time for sorrow has come to an end; do not weep but announce the Virgin's resurrection."

"Blessed art Thou, O Sovereign Lady; enlighten me with the light of Thy Son."

Unto the God-bearing disciples gathered, weeping before Thy tomb, O Virgin, Thomas did appear and speak out, saying: "Why do you number the living among the dead? For She has risen, as the birthgiver of God!"

"Glory to the Father, and to the Son and to the Holy Spirit."

We worship the Father, and His Son and the Holy Spirit: the Holy Trinity, one in essence. We cry with the Seraphim: "Holy, holy, holy art Thou, O Lord."

"Now and ever, and unto the ages of ages. Amen."

Having given birth unto the Giver of Life, Thou hast now gone unto ageless life. Rejoice, O Virgin: unto the disciples Thou didst give joy in place of sadness. On the third day Thou didst rise from the grave, O Virgin, just as did the Lord.

"Alleluia, alleluia, alleluia, glory to Thee, O God." (thrice)

III.

With wondrous strength is the Cross invested.
Its splendor nothing can excel;
Triumphantly it's manifested
On earth, in heaven and in hell.

It opens spaces infinite,
Strikes Satan with a mortal blow;
To God can man ascend with it,
With power over death below.

From the Cross a power, born of grace,
Is poured out over all the earth;
Beneath its shelter, there's no place
For sorrow to be given birth.

On it, the Giver, crucified,
Gives joy in all adversity;
And He Who had been mocked and tried
Helps those who suffer as did He.

The Cross is our support and aid
In doing something useful, good;
The strength of Jesus Christ has made
Us love as He, love's author, would.

The Cross calms fear in tribulation,
Providing us with peace of soul;
It wards off onslaughts of temptation,
Preserving virtue sound and whole.

Not only is our soul directed
To live a life of holiness,
Our body also is protected
From earth's afflictions and distress.

The Cross leaves all the tares unsown
Which Satan seeks to grow in man;
Infernal pride we thus dethrone
And turn to dust the devil's plan.

So go, my brother, with the Cross!
With zeal, upon its power call;
And if you meet with gain or loss,
Your shield it is, your guarding wall.

For he who walks with the Cross's force
And runs toward it earnestly,
As to a living water source,
Will ripen into purity.

The shadow of death he will not fear;
He'll strive for ageless light above;
To Christ, his Lord, he'll grow more near,
Then blossom out with holy love.

The Cross of Christ we rightly cherish.
With fervent hope to it we cling;
For through it we will never perish,
And from it bliss is issuing.

Fathers, mothers! Take with you
Your children to the Cross's base.
Repent and tell yourselves anew:
The Cross is God's great gift of grace!

Salvation sprung from that great Tree;
Abundant blessings it has brought;
Without the Cross, the mystery
Of our redemption would be not.

From you your children first will learn
To love the Cross they stand before,
And later they'll themselves return
To honor it for evermore.

May every child embrace with love
The Cross of Jesus Christ each day,
And may their tender hearts know of
Its strength to save them when they pray.

And in this custom may they grow
For all of Russia's benefit—
To call down grace, which God will show
To those with whom their lives are knit.

Make strong their souls, still newly born,
With work that comes from vital need;
Don't harm them with intrigues and scorn,
And thus their labors will succeed.

And through the Cross's mighty power,
Our Orthodox believing nation
Will flourish, wondrous grace will flower
And grow with each new generation.

Then God will not our land forsake,
But call it to divine election;
The world, through it, will then awake
To seek the Cross and its protection.

IV.

A monk's appeal—in his grief and temptation—to Lord Jesus

To Thee, O God, I send my plea:
Forsake me not, long-suffering Lord!
My hands are reaching out to Thee;
Thy grace alone have I implored.

Instruct me, Master, how to pray.
I walk in darkness, as one blind.
This cloud has yet to pass away—
It still casts shadows on my mind.

Disperse the darkness of temptations,
Illuminate the path within,
Raise up my fallen inclinations
And resurrect the death of sin.

I sacrificed my father, mother,
Possessions, homes. I cast aside
The love of sister and of brother:
The world to me was crucified.

Withdrawing from the world's embraces,
To deserts, mountains, woods I fled;
I settled down within these places
To see another realm outspread.

Illustration from *Russian Pilgrim*, 1913.

I only hope for God's salvation,
A harbor from the stormy sea,
That cowardice and trepidation
May, through Thy grace, depart from me.

I must regain Thee—will I ever?
Where do I look, O hidden One?
O, what a difficult endeavor
Have I, a sinner, now begun!

I was directed to the route
Which, with Thy Cross, Thou once didst choose.
Thy path of thorns was pointed out,
And, following, I left my shoes.

I walked the path—by choice, not force—
Although I labored all the while.
I thought that I had run the course,
Not having even gone a mile.

My feet were injured on the trail
As they went over rough, damp soil.
And soon my steps began to fail;
I moved with ever greater toil.

I tore my clothes in the desert's heat,
And then by thieves I was assaulted.
Thus being lowered, I entreat
Thy Name, above all names exalted.

Thou seest I have no more power;
Thy strength alone can now restore me.
I cannot see beyond this hour,
So let Thy brightness shine before me.

Creator, I shall see Thee then;
I'll know Thee, all-surpassing Mind.
I'll feel my soul revive again,
And leave my wandering behind.

My grief and sorrow I'll forget,
Forget the great adversity
Which on the rugged path I met
And which has always hindered me.

My soul, through troubles, perseveres,
But I'll arise above this pain
That I've endured so many years,
Fulfilling what Thou didst ordain.

O Savior, there is more to go;
I still have many miles ahead.
I haven't gone halfway, I know,
Along the path that Thou didst tread.

"My yoke is easy," Thou didst say,
"The burden which I bear is light."
I trust in Thee, and I obey
Because Thy word is true and right.

This pathway, through Thine intervention,
Will not be hard to walk upon;
And, staying firm in my intention,
I'll have the strength to carry on.

Though at each step there falls a tear
Which comes from loving sacrifice,
I feel at peace that I am here
And walk the road to paradise.